ACKNOWLEDGEMENTS

It took almost three years to complete writing these memoirs. Although the stories were locked away in my heart over the years, I had to find a way to get them down on paper. Thanks to my youngest daughter, Kamila we were able to bring these back to life.

I thank my wife and my entire family and friends for all the support and love I have received over the years, who have given me the courage to write down my memoirs as a series of short stories. These are filled with history, family and triumph over adversity.

It has been a pleasure writing this book and I hope it brings the reader hours of joy and intrigue.

EARLY LIFE

I was born in Barisal in 1936 on the 30th Day of August to a middleclass family. I came into the world on a strong windy night. My father used to work as an Inspector with the India General Navigation and Rivers Steamers Company during the British rule in India, 1920-1942.

My father was on an official tour auditing the Steamer Stations by the South of Bengal and was unaware of my mother's condition on that special night. There were no doctors or nurses available, no road or railway lines. The only method of communication was by ship which would take three to four days for a letter or telegram to reach the recipient. Letters would travel by ship from one port to another. He had to leave my mother in the care of family members and some maidservants. Luckily my mother had no complications during childbirth. My father came home and was delighted to find a bouncing baby boy in her arms, her first born son after two daughters. This was the beginning of my tale.

I was a happy child, living a normal life. Although I was a little boy, I remembered the incidents that happened in my childhood. Whatever I had heard, seen or have been told, I remembered them all.

NO HAIR CUTS

I remember when I was a little boy in Barisal I did not want to have my haircut. The barber used to come in every two weeks to cut everyone's hair, and I refused to have my haircut. I used to scream! My father used to sit down and take me onto his lap with an orange or a little toy in my hand. I would stop crying and let the barber cut my hair.

Sometimes I would weep and not stop weeping for a long time, so my father used to take me to the big fish tank and asked me to find out which fish I liked and which of the fishes had a pink or red colour and so on.

I would have to have a bath after the haircut and I used to cry as usual. I would ask my father silly questions, like "Where was my hair?"

"Can the Barber return my hair on my head?"

I used to say lots of funny things to my father. When I grew older and remembered this and I laughed to myself that was so funny!

FISH ON DRY LAND

Barisal Division is one of the eight administrative divisions of Bangladesh. Located in the south-central part of the country, it is was the administrative capital. Barisal city, lies in the Padma River delta on an offshoot of the Arial Khan River.

Our House was not too far from the Bay of Bengal in Barisal. I was very young, the house was fenced by bamboo sticks but was strong and sturdy. Myself and my two elder sisters Jahanara and Anawara used to play different games inside the fence and my Mother would sit on a chair in the Veranda and watch us. We would laugh and run around and cycle. Sometimes the approaching tide from the sea would disturb our play. We had to stop playing and run inside the house. We watched the floating of our toys over the flood water, it could be in the daytime or the evening depending on the time of the tide but it happened quite often. We would run and catch our toys and the fish as well! Sometimes they were caught by the cleverly placed bamboo fence. Various kinds of fish used to get in through bamboo traps made by my father. The fish entered through the holes in the bamboo traps and could not get out. They were trapped and started jumping on the dry surface of the back garden. It was such a beautiful sight and so exciting to see! I could never forget.

At some point in my adult life in 1964, I remembered this scene. When I was in Weston Super-Mare, some twenty years later I recalled the tide in Barisal. It was one of my fondest memories. At night in Weston Super-Mare I would leave the window open to hear the exciting sound of the forceful tide and with it came flooding back the memories of the sea in my childhood. The beautiful sound of the tide of Bay of Bengal.

PITHAS IN BANANA LEAVES

We were waiting for the late afternoon to come as this was the time when we used to go to Barisal every day. There was no railway line in Barisal, only the shipping line through the waters. My two sisters and myself would go accompanied by a guard to look after us. The port staff were happy to meet us, they used to buy us sweets and chocolates. We watched the ships and barges coming in and anchoring to stop to unload the cargo and the passengers from Calcutta, Bombay and Madras alighting from the ships.

It was nice to see the thatched shops by the port, selling home made butter wrapped with banana leaves and 'Pithas', a sort of snack made with steamed rice flour and coconut flakes, cool home-made yoghurt beautifully presented in earthen terracotta bowls made of clay, 'Channa Chaat' a scrumptious dish made chickpeas and chilli and tamarind. I could see fresh coconut milk dipped in cold water (in the absence of modern ice cold drinks) which made my mouth water and of course the ice lollies brought in big flasks to keep them cool which we so enjoyed. The staff from the Port used to offer us the items we loved the most.

We enjoyed the hustle and bustle of the port. When the sun was about to set and darkness appeared, we returned home with a happy mood.

LOVE FOR THE CINEMA

One day I started crying to go to the cinema. My father would not allow me to go but I was so adamant. I would not listen to anybody, not even my father. I was around seven years old, and I was too young for the show. At last reluctantly my father allowed me to go with one of the guards and my sister who was two and a half years older than me. We entered the cinema hall, the lights were off. It was so dark. We could hardly see each other. I got worried, how would we be able to see the movie without any light? It was a projection. All of a sudden I noticed the screen got brightener and came to life. I saw some people started singing a patriotic song, some words I caught were 'Love India'. Then came some advertisements and the movie started itself. The name of the film so far as I could remember was 'Kismet' which means 'Fate'.

I remember, it was about a poverty stricken theatre owner and his crippled daughter who encountered a pickpocket. I can still remember the story and the musical songs of sorrow they played within the film which meant that God was the One who created us and gives us sustenance. We live on His mercy, without which we could not survive. He is all Merciful. It had touched my mind so much that I could not forget those few lines which had been ingrained into my heart deeply. The song can be found at the following link https://www.youtube.com/watch?v=bgrLz-MrGcA.

Sometimes I remember and sing along to the song by Amirbiai Karnataki in 1943's Kismet Movie:

"ab tere siva ab tere siva kaun mera krishan kanhaiya bhagwan kinare se laga de meri naiya

ab tere siva ab tere siva kaun mera krishan kanhaiya

6

bhagwan kinare se laga de meri naiya ab tere siva

ab meri khushi ki duniya babul ne cheen li
mere sukho ki kaliya kismat ne bin li
ab meri khushi ki duniya babul ne cheen li
mere sukho ki kaliya kismat ne bin li
ab tu bacha laaz meri bansi bajaiya
bhagwan kinare se laga de meri naiya ab tere siva"

The song means, without God, who else will be there to save us?

7

FLOATING SNAKES

In 1941 when I was five years old I remember such devastation. I had a bitter experience with the floods in Bangladesh. The whole of Barisal was submerged in flood water, thousands of people lost their homes and belongings and had no where to go. Although our house was situated on a higher level in Barisal town, during the whole flood period we could not move around at all.

We were confined inside our house, we had to sleep on a bed whereby our beds were placed on the top of two other wooden beds and they moved constantly. We used to count the loose items floating by us in the water. Flood water spread all over the area, we used to see people travelling over the roads and gardens by manually propelled boats only. The miseries of the people knew no bounds. Some people used to make boats and rafts with banana trees hooked together and used as a transport to travel from one house to the other. The children enjoyed such boating.

There were snakes floating, there were garulies (a sect of people who treated people bitten by snakes). I found cooking pots and many useful items were floating in the water and many other things. Myself and my siblings used to count the floating items flowing over the flood water. I can never forget such an incident.

The risk of flood is very high in Bangladesh as 80 percent of the land is flood plain. Most of the land in Bangladesh is located less than 10 metres above the sea level and there have been many fatalities due to flood over the years.

Later, I heard a very sad story about the floods from my wife. Her elder brother Khosru who was the first child of her parents passed away at the age of seven. He was sitting on a raft made from a banana tree on top of the water and he fell in the water and drowned. Strangely he had been playing in the sand on the bank and had dug out a child's grave before he got on the raft. He was saying that he had dug out his own grave. His mother was distraught after his untimely death.

Myself and my brother Tutu, used to go to St Gregory Primary and Infant School in Barisal. It was not too far from our house so we were escorted by a guard who took us there and back. We used to pick the big tomatoes from our garden when returning home from school. They were big red juicy tomatoes, we used to eat them and fill our pockets to take some home for our sisters. When the abnormal flood was over there came the usual tidal water all over our back garden which was fenced by bamboo mats. My father tactfully kept holes in between the fence for the small fish to enter the garden fence. When the tide pulled away, we found the small fish trapped and they were jumping all around the garden! We loved chasing and catching the fish.

DRESS CODE

In the early months of 1942, my father went out for an evening walk. He saw my uncle and his friend approaching. He had arrived on a Passenger ship from Calcutta. My father was wearing '*Dhutti*' which was worn by both Hindus and Muslims alike in India.

They were engaged in talking between themselves, it was a bit noisy to the rest of the Zamidar's (land owners) of in the area. One asked his guard Shumon to look outside and find out who was walking and talking so loudly.

Shumon came to have a look and then replied "Huzoor (Sir), it was three people. A gentleman and two Muslims"

My uncle asked my father, "Why did he say a gentleman and two Muslims?"

My father explained to him, that as he was the one wearing Dhutti, he was referred to as a gentleman. As they two were both wearing Sherwani (Muslim clothing) and a topi (hat) they were called Muslims. The Dhutti was more respected and treated with a special consideration!

WORLD WAR TWO

In 1942, World War Two began. It was a horrific experience for a small boy. The memories of which are still etched on my mind today. The war aircrafts flew, one after another in the sky, the sound was so unbearable that my hands clasped over my ears. I could see the white smoke in the sky trailing after the aircrafts. I could hear the open fire and other children scrambling from the gardens into their houses screaming in fear.

Sometimes I felt frozen and did not move. I could hear the shriek of the siren, the young, old, disabled, frail and vulnerable people rushed inside the bunker underground to hide from the firing and gas. Children ran into their mother's arms and hid their faces. Smoke was all around, and the air was thick and difficult for us to breathe. Myself, with my parents ran into the underground bunker to save our lives. The rich and the poor all ran for their lives and filled the bunkers, without exception or segregation, there was no time to waste!

HOLLINGBERRY'S MANNERS

My father, had to see his boss Mr Hollingberry, the Director General of the Company for the southern region of Bengal. Going to see the Director on official business, my father knocked on the door a few times but there was no response. He then pushed the door and entered into his office. The Director stood up, shouting and had said,

"You Indian! Don't you have any manners? You didn't bother to knock and wait for permission to enter my office?".

My father replied "*I did not know that you were devoid of hearing!*"

It was some months after, Mr Hollingberry entered my father's own office without knocking himself and having no permission to enter. He entered the room. My father took a rubber hammer out of his desk drawer and shouted at him giving him exactly the same reception he had received earlier. He apologised immediately and said;

'I am sorry, I did not expect such a reply from an Indian". He also said this was the first time he saw an Indian with such guts!

A few months later, the Director called him into his office and had said,

"I have got some good news for you! You have been promoted to the post of Divisional Inspector for the southern region of Bengal (Now Bangladesh)!" after this the two became great friends. He even presented my father with his shotgun as a token of his friendship and '*His Master's Voice'* Gramophone (HMV) for the use of his children. They used to go to Sundarbon together. One of

the most beautiful hunting spots in Asia. Where people used to go for deer hunting. My father and Mr Hollingberry used to go very often to hunt Deer. They never came back empty handed and we always looked forward to their return.

THE TELEGRAM S.O.S

In October 1942 there was a critical juncture for our family.

My father received a telegram that his father; my grandfather, who was nearly 110 years old and in a critical condition. His health was deteriorating and he became bedridden. There was no-one to take the responsibility of the family lands. He needed someone to safeguard the prestige and position of the dynasty of the Chowdhury family (Land Owners), the family lands were immense and from the pre-Mughal era.

When the British took over India they retained the same 'Zamindari' (Fudal) system. Lord Cornwallis was the Governor General of India who introduced the *Permanent Settlement Act* in 1793 for India. By this Act of Parliament, the Chowdhury's retained their Title permanently and their heirs were also entitled to use the title. They had to collect revenues from their tenants and pay one fourth (Chowth) to the British Authorities. It was also agreed by the British Government that 16% of the executive Government jobs would be reserved for them alone as they came from a ruling class of family.

My father took over the responsibilities of his father and started settling down at his ancestral home at Noorpur, Fenchuganj. As he did not know much of the Zamindari system, he invited his maternal Uncle who used to spend time with my Grandfather relating to our ancestral land, the pending court cases and so on.

BACK TO ROOTS - FENCHUGANJ

He responded to his father's telegram by taking immediate leave and later resigned from his post to take responsibility for the family. He brought his family back home to their ancestral village of Fenchuganj, Noorpur. It was July 1942 and our family took the gruelling journey by a steam ship towards the Bay of Bengal and through the rivers of East Bengal.

Although I visited some places where there were steamer stations in Barisal division with my father while he was auditing the steamer stations in Bhola, Patuakhali, Jahalakati, Bagerhat and Tushkhali, but the journey to Fenchuganj was so long and arduous.

It was so dangerous for us to undertake such a risky journey during World War Two. The ship used to stop in every station for some time depending on the quantities of shipment and the cargo and passenger movements. It was a ten day journey from Barisal to Fenchuganj. The same ship used to come from Calcutta enroute via Barisal to Assam on a regular basis. It used to take less than ten days but due to the War it was taking a lot longer and delays due to checks by the Army. Myself and my younger brother Tutu used to play with handmade paper boats to pass the time. We used to throw them into the river Meghna and watch them going up and down in the waves or sinking with the tide. At night the ship anchored by the shore. We were sitting in darkness and the lights were off. We saw eachothers faces with natural light only.

We were passing under the longest bridge of Bengal called the 'Bharab Bridge'. We noticed that cannons were fitted on both sides of the bridge. The British Army were patrolling the bridge, our ship had a British Flag hoisted on the Stern of the ship. The British Army allowed us to pass through. I had two brothers and two sisters and myself, we really enjoyed the journey. Sometimes we would go to see our baby brother Zitu who was in my Mother's arms in between our games on the deck. The ship stopped at Bhairab station for nearly four hours for loading and unloading of cargo and passengers. There were fishermen on their boats which were full of fish. The most loved fish in Bangladesh was the 'Hilsha fish' which is very tasty. My father bought some fish and a special vegetable from another boat called 'Potol' which would go well with the fish curry. We had our own designated chef on the ship who cooked the curry for us and it was delicious but full of bones! My mother had to separate the bones for us on the plate. I could never forget the taste of it and remember this experience when I eat Hilsha fish today.

We saw another boat passing by, there was someone on the boat which covered with banana leaves. Some people were sitting near to it, looking very sad. My father asked the people on the boat,

*"What is in the boat you are carrying? Is it a dead body? Where are you taking it?"*A reply came from the person on the boat, *"It is the body of a person who has been bitten by a snake. It is going to a village, to a 'Bedi' or 'Garullies' who are specialists in treatment of snake bites"*.

They treat their patients in a special way to extract the poison from the body. The victims get cured completely, for good, that is if they didn't die before receiving treatment! The group of people in Bangladesh still practice this magic method of extraction of poison but the number of such practitioners are rare because of sophisticated medical treatment nowadays.

THREE TOOTS, WE'RE HOME!

The next day the Steamer had left Marculi station, it whistled three times in one go as usual to let my grandfather know that his son was coming home. He would send his people to receive us and carry our luggage. By the time we arrived at Fenchuganj, a dazzling looking steamer station, our destination. We were received warmly by our people.

On the way home we saw the river Kushiara was full of ships, barges, despatches, all anchored by the riverside. We saw a big steamer repairing workshop, a big bungalow of the Chief Engineer and a bungalow of the Pilot, the staff quarters for its engineering workers and office staff and a hospital. There were some quaint shops by the side of the road. We were amazed to see the wonderous sight of the place!

This is where the family settled for the next generation and the generations to come. Our native home was situated less than half a mile away from the Port and 15 miles from the main city of Sylhet. It took twenty days to reach the destination from Barisal to Fenchuganj.

I asked my father *"You said all the time that we come from a village at Fenchuganj but I cannot see any village around! It looked bigger and brighter than where we lived in Barisal"*.

My father said *"Just you wait and see!"*

We met all of our relatives who were awaiting eagerly to receive us all. My Great Grandfather Muhammad Hassan Chowdhury, looked different. He was standing strong like a giant apart from the others. He kissed us lovingly with enthusiasm. Having arrived home, I found a different world with a bigger home, bigger family, bigger space, wide fields to play, a very big pond in front of the house with a boat in it for fishing and enjoyable trips.

MY BONEY GRAND FATHER

I used to stay close to my Dada (Grandfather), I was his eldest Grandson and he loved me so much. He used to walk with a walking stick, I used to eat with him on a speciality made, big clay plate (Hanok). He had two prominent clavicle bones on his chest. One day I asked him why had he swallowed the bones that got stuck in his chest! He said sarcastically, "*I was hungry, that's why*". I lost my Grandmother before I was born, but I am sure she would have been just as much fun! My companionship with my Dada did not last long.

One day in the late afternoon, I was busy angling on the pond. My Grandfather who could not walk with me, was lying down on his bed. I heard everybody crying. I rushed into his room and found he had passed away. He had left us, it was just before sunset at the end of 1942.

My father became helpless. He did not know the pros and cons of land matters, its ownership, possession etc as he was not at home with his father to have learned these things. He invited his maternal Uncle who was very close to his father and had proper advice and guidance from him and learned a lot of skills in land matters and its ownership. My Grandfather was ill for a long time and had none to stand by near him. People took advantage by occupying his lands and fraudulently recorded their ownership of his land under their names without his knowledge. At this time World War Two was going on in full swing.

MILK, MILK AND MORE MILK

Whilst in Barisal we had an abundance of milk however, after reaching Fenchuganj my father noticed that we had only two milk giving cows and were not giving sufficient milk. It was only sufficient for tea, coffee and pudding but not enough for children's daily consumption. My father then bought two milk giving cows from the Indian province of Sind, far away from the district of Sylhet. They were producing plenty of milk for all sorts of consumption.

The problem was solved satisfactorily. Whilst in Barisal we used to have plenty of milk even some milk products were made regularly for the family. We had a big goat which gave plenty of milk. The goat used to follow us wherever we went, even inside the house! We used to love it as a member of our family. But here we had all sorts of vegetables growing in our fields, fish from our pond and natural lakes and canals as our family did not charge any money from the fishermen. It was a common practice.

THE ENCHANTED HORSE

We had a beautiful brown horse at home. As I was very young I had to put the horse under a guava tree. I climbed the tree and jumped to mount the horse on its back! Many people outside the village tried to ride the horse but it wouldn't allow anyone apart from us. They were thrown off its back. One day it let someone ride it and after a while threw him into a lake and off he went! I wanted it to go faster but it would not. It might have thought that I was not used to high speed and he was careful with me. After I grew slightly, he would take me faster and faster. One day he threw me on a bush! He did not run away, he stood by me and started licking me like we were playing a game. It seemed like we could talk to each other.

When I got used to it, I began to race with another horse belonging to a local police sergeant. Our horse was called 'Nicky', my father would take him wherever he went. He would ride him everywhere. It was that time where there were not many built up roads like today, only the pathways between the farmland. Bangladesh (East Pakistan) was a land of many rivers and canals going from one place to the other was by manually propelled boats. The rivers and canals had to be crossed by ferryboats and our horse Nicky was so used to it that it could easily ride on the wooden made ferry boat to cross the river accompanied by my father or his stablehands. Even now when I see a horse it reminds me of Nicky.

RESIGNATION NOT ACCEPTED

The peaceful condition did not last very long for my father as he decided to stay in his paternal home and resigned from his job. But Mr Hollingberry did not accept his resignation. He wanted him back on the job, but it was not possible to do that, because of the promise he made to his father to take care of the land and family and community matters.

Mr Hollingberry then offered him a new position as Port Commissioner in Chittagong Port which was an international Sea Port and the biggest port in Bengal. My Father still refused to join. My Mother and two Elder sisters and myself insisted him to accept the new offer but my father flatly refused. He said,

"Do you want our prestige and position to go down? And we become subservient to the so-called power seekers? No, I would not let it happen. I want the prestige of our family above all"

My father realised that he needed more cash money to deal with greedy insurgents who wanted the downfall of our family heritage. He was determined to deal with them. He would have to take many cases to court to rightfully claim our lands from people who were trying to claim them as their own after the death of my grandfather. There were many village feuds to deal with and only my father could do it.

THE DIL (HEART) OF THE MOUNTAINS

He went to Margaretta in Assam. He got acquainted with the British Military General responsible for the 'Assam' province of India which was the strong hold of the British in the East in World War Two, a friend of Mr Hollingberry, the General was pleased to meet him.

He entrusted him with a contractual job. My father began building war shelters and hospitals in Margaretta. He was entrusted with the job of building a 200-bedded emergency hospital, a number of bunkers and shelter homes in mountainous area. He immediately came home and recruited many trustworthy and able handed people amongst his tenants who worked tirelessly for him in building the proposed military project. The General was so pleased he used to call him "*The Dil (Heart) of the Mountains*" as his name was Dilawor Hussain Chowdhury, in recognition of his services for the British Military Projects in Assam. My father earned a fortune.

After the world war II was over, he came back to settle in his paternal home and was welcomed by some people as an heir of his father Hassan Chowdhury. He got involved with village politics wholeheartedly and was determined to fight against the insurgents and others who took advantage of my Grandfather's illness. He wanted to follow his father's footsteps and fight in court for justice against those people. He dealt with many court cases mostly of a serious nature, but he survived. The rival group either individually or jointly came to apologise to him directly and joined him accepting him as the de facto landowner of the Pargona. His power, honesty and sincerity impressed them and they elected him as the Sarpanch (Village Head) several times. His union council became a role model in (East) Pakistan and he was awarded The Best Chairman Award by Ayub Khan the President of Pakistan in 1956.

STEALING PUMPKINS

I was a boy full of joy. I used to run home from school through the beautiful green paddyfields, they held cows, sheep and so many animals. I did not see such a sight in my city life in Barisal. I used to play football, kopati and other games with the boys from school, we lived a normal village life like everyone else. Life was very simple at home. However we did get into mischief a few times!

One day with two other cousins of mine we were playing in the empty green fields. There were cows, ships and a few horses were grazing in the fields. I never saw this in the town life in Barisal. It was so amazing I noticed that hundreds of birds were sitting on the top of the bamboo trees singing cheerfully.

I had a Dodallu (a special handmade sling shot) to shoot with a clay made marble-like ball. Sometimes a few birds flew away but if aimed properly I shot them and they fell on the ground. There were competitions to catch them between the children. We enjoyed it immensely as some fun and games. The field was covered with yellow flowers from mustard plants. It looked so beautiful. The other side of the field had plenty of vegetables growing over the land. The river Kushiara flows through and you can see the boats, the steam ships and barges plying through. There was a ferry boat.

We were thinking of crossing the wild river to view the other side of the river. They did not charge any money for they knew who we were. We crossed the river and found a lot of vegetables growing everywhere. Namely, pumpkins, marrows, melons, peanuts, mustard and many more. We thought it would be fun if we take one pumpkin each home, so we did. On the way home we realised that everyone at home would scold us if they did not belong to us. They must have been stolen by us! We hid them in a big basket. We heard the voice of a woman complaining to my mother that three boys form this house had stolen pumpkins from their farmland.

Just before she finished, her husband appeared and had said,

"*The boys did not steal the pumpkins it was theirs! I cultivated the pumpkins on their land*" and thus we were saved!

They were tenants of our land who cultivated fruits and vegetables on it. They let it pass.

CLEAN WITH COW DUNG

I remember one day, while going to school, my Mother asked me to drop the laundry to the washerman's house. My cousin was with me. He was standing at the front of the house and I entered inside to drop the washing off. The wife of the washerman started screaming!

She said *"Ram Ram, why did you enter inside my house?"* I told her I came to drop the washing. She said, I made the house dirty, I should not have entered the house. *"You should have called us to collect the washing, now I have to clean the house!"* she took the laundry away and immediately started to purify the room with cow dung paste mixed with water and spread all over the floor!

I said, *"It is you who is making the room dirty with the cow dung"* but she kept quiet. I came back home and told my Mother the whole story. She then told me, a Muslim should not enter a Hindu house even though you are the son of their landowner, you are a Muslim. That is why she was cleaning it with the cow dung which is their sacred animal and cow dung was purer than a Muslim! I was so surprised by this. I said to my Mother, *"How can a Muslim be more impure than cow dung?"* I really did not understand.

The next day, the husband of the woman came to apologise for the incident that happened. I said to him, *"I'm Sorry, I entered your house without knowing your traditions"*.

He said, *"You are not supposed to apologise to me, I am here to apologise to you"*. In those days the Hindus treated Muslims differently. But he was embarrassed that his wife had spoken to me in that way as we were the land owners of the area.

VISITING NANA AND NANU

We used to go to our Nana's (Maternal Grandfather's) home which was at least twenty miles away from our village home. It would take around 8 hours without proper communication lines we would have to travel by a wooden made manually propelled boat to the railway station. The train journey to Sylhet was 45 minutes but the trains were not very frequent during the war time. There were two trains only a day used to arrive very late everyday. The train was usually full of soldiers. There would have been not much space left for the use of the general public. Besides, there were strong military security personnel who needed to check all the luggage, small or big, for the 'open and show checks'.

Some soldiers were extremely rude and behaved so roughly that we were frightened. We cried and sometimes screamed out of fear, but that was not allowed. But one thing was good about them, when the train was moving a bit faster then normal, they used to throw peanut bags or containers to the village children who were running alongside the train.

We arrived at Sylhet station, we had to hire a boat which was being checked again by the soldiers. We had to have some dry food with us so that we did not feel hungry in this journey which could have been delayed for hours for any unforeseeable reason.

We had to go through the river Surma where all the steam ships either on their voyage or anchored on the riverbank, we had to carry on until we reached our destination.

FISH TRADERS

Fenchuganj was famous for its fish trade. Different kinds of fish were available during the seasons. During the Summer season the Hilsha fish, Rohu, Boush, Rayya, Lasso, Rani and many other kinds of fish were available. We did not have to buy fish normally from outside. We had our own ponds, natural lakes and other sort of fisheries for daily consumption. But we did buy the seasonal river fish from the passing by fishermen's boats at the Kushiara river. The taste of the fresh water seasonal fish was mouth watering.

Fish from Fenchuganj were exported to all parts of Bengal for which it was necessary to have a railway station called Maisgo within one mile distance. Both the stations, Fenchuganj and Maisgo have carried on transport links today starting from the British rule in India.

*

MALHOKIA SPINACH PICKING

During the monsoon period sometimes we used to make a trip to visit our Khala (mother's sister) by boat during our school holidays. Our country Bangladesh, formerly known as East Pakistan; was full of rivers, canals and national lakes. There was water everywhere, as far as we could see. There were not many roads at that time. Everywhere we went it was by boat only, like cars nowadays. The fields, the paddy lands, were covered with jut plants within which there was a narrow passage like space for a boat to pass through.

The owners wanted the top of the jut plants to be taken off (pruning) by the people on the boats so that it grows taller and grows more juts. So we would take the top part of the Jut plant every time we passed through and it would be used as spinach or vegetable. It is one of the tastiest and nutritious vegetable dishes of Bengal cooked with fresh garlic and ginger referred to as Naali Saag (Malhokia), available nowadays as a frozen vegetable in some shops. A slippery vegetable like okra (lady's fingers).

FILTHY BLOOD SUCKERS

While at home I found an exciting event was going on. That was fishing by many people in a big natural lake in front of our home which belonged to my family along with other lakes and lands. We used to sell the other lakes but this one was reserved for our tenants to catch fish once a year in front of our home so that the women in the house could see for themselves and enjoy the fun. The fishing was free. That tradition had been carried on from the time of our forefathers (Free-fishing). The people were so excited, they always looked forward to this event each year. I was only a little boy, I could not stop myself. I jumped into the lake to catch fish, I got hold of a small fishing net which was given by a man. I started using it when another boy of my age joined me as I did not know how to use the fishing net.

When in the muddy water, I felt some sort of itching on my thigh. I just ignored it for a while, but the itching sensation increased more. I touched it and I felt something slippery! I got up to the shore and looked at my leg. I found a big fat leech was stuck to my thigh sucking my blood at random, the blood was running down my thigh. I got frightened and screamed loudly. The people who were fishing took the leech out. They then burned a rug and put the ashes on my injury. The rolling of the blood then stopped from my leg. I went home crying and showed it to my Mother. She had it cleaned with warm water and put some cream and bandaged the place. Since then, I never went fishing this way. It was a bitter lesson for me I had learned the hard way, which I would never forget.

NOWKA DOWR - BOAT RACE

In every year at Fenchuganj, on the river Kushiara on the very day of Doshera (which is the festival day of the emergence of the Hindu Goddess, Durga) there used to be a famous boat race. People from all over Bengal came excitedly to enjoy the race. This had been arranged by the Chief Executive of India General Navigation Company Ltd with his associates at the Fenchuganj boat race (Nowka Dowr).

At the boat race some skilled boat men from all over Bengal used to take active part in the race. Thousands of spectators used to enjoy the special race, from tea garden owners to top civil servants, many people used to come the enjoy the exciting event. All the boats were decorated with different colours and uniformed rowing staff. They used to sing exciting Hindi and Bengali songs loudly with drums rolling and kartals (Indian musical plates). At the Bow there were men standing in the guise of jokers, monsters, ghosts, monkeys etc, dancing wildly with loud music. It was such an exciting sight for people of all ages to see. The spectators at the river bank enjoyed snacks of various kinds, namely, Peas, Bombay mix, Samosas, Chana Choor, Sweetcorn and lots of homemade Indian snacks and sweets and of course candy floss for the children! There was paan supari as a treat for everyone. We had so much fun!

The Chief Executive of the Company gave away prizes to the winners of the boat race. The race was held every year on the Doshera day by the river and people looked forward to this special fun day event for families. It was unique of its kind, I had never seen a boat race of this kind before, or after, in England I attended races in

Birmingham, London, Stratford Upon Avon, but it was not the same enthralling experience I had been accustomed to in Fenchuganj.

Right opposite the snack stalls, I found hundreds of people surrounded in circles and a couple of boys dressed like young girls! They were dancing to wild music and with funny colourful dress promoting the sale of newly produced 'Biri' (Indian homemade Cigarettes). They were dancing and singing to famous Indian songs, singing..

"Maya Colcutta ase leye ayyee ekush biri namm, nitay bhulona re moyna, khete bhulo na, ekush biri naam tar"

(Oh my Indian brothers, listen to me, we brough lovely cigarettes from the city of Calcutta, manufactured very carefully. Do not forget to buy and take the luxurious item named '21 Cigarette').

Oh it was so funny! I still remember their song and the funny dance!

A BUCKET FULL OF MANGOES

My father was a good cultivator of fruit within the boundaries of our home. When I used to come home after the exams were over, and during holidays, I did not want to make friends with others. I spent a lot of time with my father. I used to help him in planting the fruit trees, like mangoes, jackfruit, pineapple, papaya, and many other tropical fruit trees. He said to me that he had seven sons who eventually have seven wives who would find sticks and pluck the fruits from the trees!

He said, "*How nice it would be. I would watch them through the window, my daughter in laws will go out in the garden for some fresh air in the evenings and pluck the fruits together in a joyous mood*". He simply could not wait.

Years later when the trees were full of ripe fruits, my brother-in-law Faisal Bhai, a close friend of mine came to visit us. He was surprised to see the view of the garden with the ripe mangoes hanging down. We both went to pluck them, he had a bucket full of mangoes! Excitedly I called my Mother to come out and see those. It was such good fun! True to my father's words, a few of the ladies of the house came out and plucked the mangoes from the trees, laughing and giggling with each other. This time it was my Mother who watched from the window.

BANDITS IN CHITTAGANJ

My Mother and siblings decided to go for a short holiday to Chittaganj Hilltrack area. We had a wipon carrier like a big jeep car. It was my Uncle's official vehicle. We went on a tour and journeyed from Sylhet to Chittaganj, it was not bad at all, except for when we reached the Hilltrack area. It was really hilly and bumpy, the car jerked from side to side, there were jungles surrounding us. A group of people appeared out of the jungle, they stood right in front of our vehicle and caused us to make an emergency stop.

There were seven of them, they were fully armed with rifles and gear. They demanded to seize all of our valuables, jewellery, cash money, wrist watches, bangles, and any other items of value. We were terrified at this and surrounded to their demands. We did not move a muscle in fear. My Mother and sisters had not brought any valuables with them and would not have brought them on a journey although we travelled with armed guards. We call these bandits 'Dacoits'.

We had some cash money, my cousin brother told us to pay them off and not escalate matters. But they were not happy at all and instead made a grab for everything we had at gunpoint. Luckily they did not physically harm us and let us go. We reached our relatives in the main land in Chittganj instead of continuing through the hilltracked area, but we were empty handed.

We stayed at my Uncle's house comfortably for two or three days as a holiday and then started the journey back home apprehensively. I still remember the horrifying incident, I was only around ten years of age at the time. Later on when I was in secondary school, I used to travel on my own by train and my Mother used to give some cash money in notes sewed into my jumper to ensure my money was not taken by others!

I WANT MY FINGER BACK

One day my younger brother Tutu was playing in a cottage-like house which was made of earthen floor with a corrugated sheet on the roof. The house was specially made for rice hulling manually in those days. Rice hulling was a process which started with the collecting of the rice paddy from the fields, then it must be laid out to dry in the sunlight. Then the cows walk over the rice grains in a circle like fashion to separate the grains. Then the grains are dried again. After this process the grains are taken to the manual Pestle and Mortar to remove the outer husks of the grains of rice. Throughout the past it was the practice of the day, the system was called 'Dehki' Husking.

My brother was only two years younger than me; he was a very mischievous child. He was by nature quite funny, restless and inquisitive. He would do any mischievous things for pleasure! He wanted me by his side as his assistant while I thought I was the Elder one and he had to listen to me! That was my attitude. But he did not take care. He started playing with a sharp knife to trim a bamboo stick. whilst playing, he suddenly chipped off the top of his left point finger, which dropped right into a mouse hole! He started crying loudly as the blood dripped down from his finger,

He exclaimed *"I want my finger back!"*.

Everyone ran to the house from the main building to see the commotion. I was standing next to him and found he was bleeding badly and asked me to bring his finger back from the mouse hole. With his bleeding finger he still went to get a shovel to dig the hole.

I said "*Stop it, you won't find it, it has gone deep into the hole*".

He said, "*You don't know anything! You don't care for me at all*".

I did not want to argue with him in case he would do something silly. The part of the finger was never found and got lost in the mouse hole. One of my Uncles came along and bandaged his finger.

THE GUARDIAN LEOPARD

My Fufu (Father's sister) used to live in another house next to ours. It was a little quieter than ours. My Father very often used to go there to rest after dinner. One night he was having a rest at Fufu's house and I was sitting beside him. It was about 10pm, my Fufu was getting ready for prayers and doing Wudu by the back door, leaving the door open for fresh air. It was dark, there was no electricity at that time.

Suddenly we heard that she was talking to someone saying "*Stop it! Don't disturb me! I am doing Wudu for prayer*"

We were so surprised, who was she talking to? There was no body there at this time of the night.

My Father asked my Fufu with a loud voice, "*Who are you talking to?*" but she kept quiet for a few seconds. Then she told us it had been a wild cat. "It comes sometimes to joke with me! It touches my hand and causes a disturbance whilst I do my wudu".

My father immediately got up and took his shot gun to take a shot at it. When he saw a leopard walking away without making a sound. My Fufu yelled, *"Stop! don't shoot at it! It doesn't cause any harm to anyone"*. She told us it stays in the bushes as a guard to us and is extremely loyal. It just jokes with her when she is getting ready from prayers!

My Father laughed with her, she said it was not joke! *"It was only joking with me! It always does"*. My Father, her younger brother did not say a word. When I told my Mother she was not surprised by this at all. She already knew the presence of the Leopard and its jokes with her sister in law. Our house was situated in a small mountain surrounded by the woods. It was not heavily populated and we had a lot of funny stories there!

THE BENCH

I was very happy at home coming back from Barisal enjoying my life in different ways as a free child, running and playing in the wide field, extracting the sugar cane juice with my teeth! It came from the sugar cane sticks. I climbed lychee trees, did fishing and angling, swimming, boating, riding, wrestling with other children of my age, flying kites and playing in the mud. Life in the village was full of fun. I thought I would not have to move anywhere. I would not go back to a town life again where people lived like birds in a cage!

But it turned out to be different when my uncle came to take me away to like in Shilchor, a town in Assam where he was a Deputy Commissioner before the independence of India. I was only nine years of age, I had to leave my parents and the freedom I had once enjoyed in my childhood, leaving my close family behind.

In 1945 My Uncle came to Fenchgang to visit. He took me away with him to live in Shilchor town in Assam with the intention that he would ultimately send me for further education in the University of Alighor in India which used to be called "*The Oxford of the East*" by the British at that time. He had arranged an admission test for me in the government high school which has some seats reserved for the children and dependents of the top government service holders. I had the test in English only and I passed and was accepted in class four in secondary school.

I became very lonely, I used to think I had none in the world. I was so sad, I was crying I said I wanted to go home. My Uncle consoled me saying when you grow up you will go home. So every day in the morning without fail are used to run to the Veranda where there was a bench for the orderly to sit on awaiting a call from my Uncle. I

38

would rush there every morning and lie down on the bench to find out whether I had grown.

It was a big family and a lot of people were living in that house. My aunt, three Cousin sisters, one cousin brother, a teacher and a religious teacher I did not know anybody. I could not mix with anybody they were of different ages, all older than me apart from one of my cousins who was younger than me. I felt like I was an intruder. Nobody loved me, everybody hated me, some used to say my Uncle had brought a stray, somebody useless.

Some said I was not good enough for education and that I didn't even look intelligent. Some said when I grow up I would only be an office boy.

I was so lonely, and helpless, I used to see myself as unworthy of everything as if there was no purpose to live in this world which was so unkind to me.

SUBMERGED IN FLOOD

A few weeks after my arrival, there was a flood in Shilchor. The whole district flooded! People where in huge distress. The river Borak, the wildest and longest river in the Assam province flooded the town and its vicinity. It was a terrible situation. Houses, offices, parks, schools, colleges were all submerged in water. I saw thatched houses, empty boats, bamboo trees and furniture were being carrying away in the vast water.

I saw monkeys jumping from bamboo to bamboo and they were having oblivious fun in this calamity. I also saw calves, goats and animals being carried away by the current much to their owner's dismay. I watched all these from the top floor of our house. This reminded me of the flood I had experienced in Barisal. Bangladesh was a country that suffered severe floods, each year floods cover 18% of the land, sometimes reaching 75% in sever cases, many lose their homes and lives due to this natural disaster.

There were three families which took shelter in our house, bringing the total occupants to 32 people! Even in such tough times, people were brought together in a sense of community. The women were cooking most of the time, the children enjoyed themselves in the flood water with boats made of banana trees. We were rowing here and there even in the downstairs rooms which were flooded with water. It was our daily routine.

The men were busy salvaging and repairing. We did not understand the severity of the situation at our age. I was very frightened to see the snakes floating over the water and I screamed, expecting someone to come and save us, but nobody came. There was water everywhere. The vigorous flood latest around two weeks. The poor people suffered the most. They took shelter in schools and in small houses in higher levels. Belongings, food, accommodation, cattle, and clothing were lost.

There was also an outbreak of cholera, pneumonia and other diseases due to the dirty water and unsanitary conditions.

THE LONELY BOY

The official residence of my uncle situated very near to the bank of the river Borak. I saw a lonely boy of around 12 or 13 years of age on a boat sweeping along the tide. He was singing a song in Monipuri (Assami) language with a melancholy tone which could be translated in plain English as

'Oh the traveller of a distant land, please take me with you, I can not live lonely in this wide world, I have been left alone'.

I used to run past the river to try and catch a glimpse of his face but never could reach the bank fast enough as the flow of the river tide was faster than I thought.

It touched my heart so deeply, he said in his own language *"Oh dur ka musafir, hum ko bi saat ley ley re, hum rehgaye akele"*

I would never forget this boy. I felt just like he did, in a foreign place, so lonely. My condition was exactly the same, in a foreign place, the pain of separation and loneliness the little boy had suffered longing to see his mother. It was as if he was begging mother nature, to take him away from the cruel world back to his mother. I also wanted to return home to my mother and siblings. But my Uncle said I have to be big enough, so I kept going back to measure myself on the bench.

WATER GODDESS - DEWLA

It was a tradition of the land owners, especially from the Sylhet region to have a big pond in front of the ancestral home 'Bari'. Back at home, the original ancestral home (puran bari) became too small for our growing family. My father decided to move to a nearby plot of land to build a purpose-built house for the new generation. With this in mind he started excavating a big pond first in front of the proposed home. The part of the land assigned for excavating the pond had a natural lake on one side which was never dry, even in the winter it was always full of water. It was full of somewhat like wild watery shrubs beneath which there was very clean water.

Some of the villagers used to think that it was a tank of the Water Goddess (Dewla) so they did not use the water for any purpose. It was believed by some people that a floating lamp on a saucer used to float on the water at midnight every day. Nobody went near it, nobody . dared to step on the lake for fishing. It was a myth. My father did not care a straw for these thoughts.

The digging of the work was completed back in 1946. At that time I became quite ill in Silchor. I was completely bedridden with a high temperature and I had no courage to tell anyone in the family about my health condition. I was so scared and helpless. At one point I recall hiding under the huge steps of a building so no one could find me. My Uncle was waiting in the car to take me to school. My family members began looking for me and found me under those huge steps. I was found with a high temperature and limp. My uncle took me straight to bed. The Chief Medical Officer of the district called in to see me at my Uncle's request and he prescribed a myriad of medications, took my blood and urine for testing but came back with no diagnosis. My uncle called quite a few other medical practitioners and no reason could be found for my illness. I was completely bedridden for around three months and could not even stand on my feet. All of a sudden my father arrived from Margaretta Assam to take me to my mother in Fenchuganj, some six hours journey by tram from where we were living.

SHEFA – THE CURE

After returning back home to my Mother, my condition gradually got worse and the doctors were baffled. They had no clue what sort of illness or disease it was. A lot of people came to see me to visit when I was sick. I was coming in and out of consciousness and I saw a little girl like an Angel standing in front of me with other visitors. I thought I heard her name being called out as Shefa (Cure). I did not think much of it at the time. Later on when I married my wife on 20 December 1965 I found that my wife's name is Shefa, the little girl has the same appearance. I remembered seeing her but she was not even born at the time of my illness so the girl was actually a vision. This is an amazing fact. I still wonder today whether that was an illusion or a vision. Perhaps it was a sign that I would recover when all hope was lost.

My Uncle could not wait anymore for me to get better, as there was no improvement in sight. At last after a few more weeks enduring this, my Uncle reserved a private ambulance from Silchor, some three hundred miles distance to where I was in Fenchuganj. He secured admission for me in the Royal Military Hospital in Shillong, a part of the Assam province and a further 400 miles from Fenchuganj. The hospital was exclusively for Military personnel and top civil servants and their dependents. I spent some five weeks there alone. For the first few days I was not given any medication to allow to test to commence.

I was under observation and tests of different kinds, after that I was given medication. I was not told what kind of medication it was as I was only a child. I believed it was a magic potion!

Miraculously I became fully cured after having the medication, I started riding the wooden horse in the hospital placed in the children's ward. I felt better than ever. I was brought back home to my Uncle's house in Silchor but to my dismay I had missed the end of year exam for my class and had to stay in the same class for another year.

THE WATER GODDESS STRIKES AGAIN

During my illness, back at home, the digging of the pond was completed. People started drawing water from the new pond for the purpose of drinking and other uses. At this time some people having superstitious beliefs came to my father and had said that some of the elder people amongst them had a dream that the God of water (a hindu belief) wanted my father's eldest son (me) because he had dug the pond. If he did not agree to surrender his eldest son to the God of the water he would take his eldest son away for good. My father did not believe in such a cock and bull story and flatly refused to comply with the wishes of their God. They dispersed broken hearted saying, they have said what they had to say. This is during the time I was very sick, but I recovered and am alive and well today!

After 18 years of my recovery from illness, in 1965 the same thing happened to my Brother Oyes. He became ill but in a different way. He was sporty and used to play football, tennis and other games in secondary school. Suddenly he became ill, he looked like a healthy normal boy but he became so weak and could not walk without any support from someone holding him up and stayed in bed most of the time. I was living in the UK and I went to Bangladesh for his medical treatment.

Both my father and myself saw many specialist doctors. Some medical professionals advised to admit him into a government mental hospital in Pabna in North Bengal because they could not diagnose any disease. Nobody could predict the chances of this recovery. His condition became talk of the town. At this time again some people who believed in superstition came to my father with the proposal of letting him go to the God of Water (Dewla).

Basically let him die slowly without any medical or treatment. To surrender to God's wish. But my father, mother including myself did not agree. The people said that God will not spare his life as we refused for the second time. The Water God will not spare his fate. My mother was a pious lady, she always after regular prayers, prayed for her beloved son and his recovery. She believed whole heartedly, "*God loves those who put their trust in Him. It is He who listens to the distressed soul and relieves its sufferings*".

It was with the divine mercy of God the All Merciful as I believed, my brother recovered completely. He is alive and well and a successful businessman and a Justice of The Peace in the UK leading a normal flourishing life.

MOTHERLAND

On my return from Shillong Robert Hospital to Shilchor. I started going to school, I remained in the same class since my illness and could not attend the annual examination. I found political turmoil, riots broke out between the Hindus and Muslims.

India began to divide its providences and became independent. The district of Silchor in Assam where I lived, fell into India. Fighting, hatred and abuse broke out in all parts of the country including Calcutta and other cities. Hindus and Muslims turned against each other and students took to the streets with slogans to protest. The Hindus were in support of Indian and the Muslims were in support of Pakistan. Confusion, hate crimes and anarchy prevailed everywhere and brother turned against brother. It was a horrific sight, screams, fire, explosions, blood filled the streets. People were trampled upon and children lost their parents in the stampede. You could almost taste the blood in the air.

I recall a happy moment seeing some college students write a slogan, '*Hindus and Muslims are brothers, we are the sons of Adam and Eve, Stand United, Stop the Fight*', but there was no one to take heed of this. No one cared. It was a state of complete anarchy. Even underage boys had to take part in the processions. Both hindus and muslims lost their motherland, birth place and the ancestral homes. It was devastating. They lost access to their parents, brothers and sisters, relatives and friends. They did not know the whereabouts of their families and kin.

There was chaos all around. The Hindus wanted their favourite land to be India and the Muslims wanted their part to be Pakistan. Lord Mount Batten the governor of

India, divided India into two states on 14th August 1947. The divided some areas on the basis of general plebiscite (election) and some places by boundary commission. Some Hindu populated areas became part of Pakistan and some heavily populated Muslim areas became part of India e.g Calcutta where the majority were Muslims because India. So also Behar and some other provinces and cities.

Fighting between both the ethnic groups started almost everywhere. Confusion, anarchy, lawlessness, hatred between both sides prevailed everywhere. I remember I was only a young boy I had to join the procession wearing a green cap marked with a moon and a star for

Pakistan. Within this period the two states gained its ground as a result many cities and district headquarters where there majority was Hindu became Pakistan and places where Muslims were the majority became India. As a result neither the Hindus nor the Muslims were happy. Eventually both lost their Motherland in the divide. People unknown to each other refused to provide food and shelter to each other. They were driven out of their country. They were split, shelterless in both the states.

THE GREAT DIVIDE

India was divided into Pakistan and India. Bangladesh had not appeared yet which would eventually be formed out of Pakistan. It was divided in such a way that the state of Pakistan was in two parts, West Pakistan and East Pakistan the distance between the two wings of Pakistan was 1000 miles. In between the two wings of Pakistan, the whole demographic area of the land including Assam province was the State of India. Both wings had a different language! If you look on the world map you will see that (West) Pakistan and East Pakistan (later renamed Bangladesh after 1971) are on two different sides on India. At that time dispute the geographic distance, it was the same country divided into two parts.

In West Pakistan, they spoke Urdu, they ate chapati (flat bread) and wore long shirts and trousers. The East Pakistanis (later called Bangladeshis) spoke Bengali and ate rice and mostly fish and wore the traditional Sari and longhi. But one thing was common, the religion of Islam was the majority. The Hindus were pleased but the Muslims were not, however all had to accept the unavoidable political situation. As a result animosity broke out between Pakistan and India continued for years.

The Government gave the option to Hindu and Muslim Government Officials who were the only ones to choose India or Pakistan respectively based on their choice of religion or ethnicity. My Uncle as a Muslim, opted to go to Pakistan to serve under the provincial government. Shilchor, where we were living had become part of India by the method of boundary commission therefore my Uncle chose to be transferred. I had to go and see my parents before leaving for Habiganj, luckily my uncle arranged a young man to accompany me throughout the journey home to Fenchuganj (which had also become part of Pakistan).

When we arrived at a railway junction called Karimganj, we saw a group of people chasing another group. They had beard, white hats on their heads and wore long shirts (Kameez), they were grabbed by the other group of people who made them sit on the streets and shaved one side of their heads forcibly and the other side of their beard and started kicking them they fell to the ground. They were gravely injured, they started crying helplessly out of fear. Nobody came to their rescue, I suppose they were Muslims, supporters of Jamiat-e-Islam-e-Hind (Muslims of India). They

had their families and homes in India. When we arrived at Kulara Junction I found the Muslims ransacked a Hindu tea stall on the railway platform. Nobody asked any question, nobody bothered to take any action or help. There were many such incidents likewise and even in bigger forms.

A CRAFTY BOY

My uncle was transferred to Habiganj as a Senior Deputy Commission and District Magistrate and Collector. I had to go with him to Habiganj and was admitted in Class VI in Habiganj Govt. School. I was good at other subjects, but very weak in Maths. My uncle engaged a private tutor who used to come at our house to teach me maths. At that time teachers, used to cane their students who were weak in any subject. I was a child of that nature. I could not do the simple mathematics in correct form and I had no interest as such in maths. My teacher used to cane me everyday!

It was so painful, being hit by a wooden cane. One day I wrapped a towel around my left arm under my jacket. So that when he would cane me, I would to extend that arm towards him to protect myself. One day he noticed that I was not exclaiming in pain, although he hit me very hard. He then asked me to take my jacket off and he asked me to show my arm; I did so. He found that I had wrapped a towel around my arm and that was why it did not hurt me! I took it off on his order and he started to hit me mercilessly with a bigger cane. It was so painful I could not forget the brutal punishment I received on that day.

One day I remembered that I saw him in Shilong. I said to my teacher,

"Sir, I remember you. I saw you in Shilong, Robert Hospital, your little daughter had an operation and we both were in the same children's ward".

He said, "Oh I remember you now".

I said "I used to play with her and had shown kindness to her. She introduced me to you as her good friend. Why could you not show some kindness to me, now?".

53

He said "*You are a crafty boy, now I know you except some kindness from me in return*". But I did not get the chance to receive that kindness or any sympathy from him. My uncle was transferred again after two years. He could not stay more than three years in one place as the British rule applied.

RUNAWAY TRAIN

A few days after, my brother Tutu who was two years younger than me; joined me in Habiganj. We then planned to run away from my Uncle's house as he was a man of very strict personality and very tough by nature, but he was very kind and loving in heart. We planned to go away somewhere to live peacefully. We were so young we did not think of the consequences. We argued between ourselves, who would go first. But nothing was decided. One day when we came back from school we found a close companion of my father had come to the house.

He asked me, *"Do you want to go home?"*

I said *"Yes!"* without thinking of anything else. I ran to change my school uniform and asked my brother Tutu not to tell anyone of my running away.

I came out with him and got onto the Hackney Carriage to the Railway Station, he bought me a packed lunch and I was feeling so happy! I was just looking forward to meeting my parents again. It was around 10 'O'Clock at night by the time I had reached Fenchuganj railway station. I was a young teenager. It was just one mile away from my home. He wanted to know whether I wanted to go home at night or would like to stay in the restaurant flat upstairs. I stayed over there. The next morning I was served a lovely breakfast at the restaurant and I went home.

When I arrived home I found my father getting ready to go out somewhere. When I saw him, realisation stuck me! I realised that I had fled from my Uncle's house, I would not have done it if I had understood the gravity of my actions before. I only saw a glimpse of my father when I realised this and I ran to my cousins house out of fear in case my father would scold me and send me back immediately.

My father said to my mother, "*I have seen Khoka (my nickname) running away*".

My mother said "*That's impossible! He cannot come in the early hours of the morning from Habiganj, it's a four hour train journey from our home!*"

He replied, "*I have seen him with my own eyes*". He sent a servant to find me, who eventually found me hiding behind a big wooden chest. He drew me out and took me home. My father, when he saw me, was not angry. He pretended to be glad to see me back!

Sarcastically he said "*Good Job you came home voluntarily, I would buy another pair of bullocks (male cows) and you could plough the fields along with other cultivators and I would save some money. Would you like to do that?*"

I said sorry, I could not do that!

My father said "*Then you better go back to your Uncle's with a letter from me and stay with him and finish your studies*". From that moment onwards, I never fled again. I wanted to become someone educated, intelligent and prestigious, not a cultivator. Although I had gone through many problems and obstacles in the past. I had a renewed sense of determination.

On my arrival back at Habiganj, I found Police Officers in a meeting with my Uncle about my absence. By this time I reached there and handed over the letter to my Uncle, I did not know what the contents were, but my Uncle became quiet. He just said, don't do that again. I did not realise how much my Uncle loved me, until I found out he considered me as his own son.

THE SCHOOL TRIP

When I was a student at Habiganj high school in 1948 a school trip to Lashkarpur was arranged. I was around 12 years old at the time.

I agreed to go there with the students of my class. We went on a bus trip to Lashkarpur which was around 14 miles away from Habiganj town. When we arrived there, we all washed and freshened up in a very large lake like a pond in front of a big dilapidated old-fashioned mansion. We sat by the pond with our teacher Mr Saleh Ahmed who gave an outline of the history of the invasion of Hazrat Shahjalal with his 360 disciples in the year 1303 AD. He told us about Syed Nasiur Uddin, Sipahsalar (General) the conqueror of Taraf Kingdom of Habiganj. After the invasion of Srihatta (Sylhet) defeating King Gaur Govinda, Hazrat Shahjalal sent his most trusted General Syed Nasiur Uddin, Sipahsala to defeat King Achak Narayan to take over Taraf, by the order of Alauddin Khilji, the ruler of India in Delhi. The Sipasalar with his Lashkar's (Soldiers) encamped in a village called later as Lashkarpur. They took over the Kingdom, defeating the King and started ruling as the new King until he decided to go back to his original mission to preach Islam in the region. As such he gave up Kingship and came back to Lashkarpur where he had been living with his soldiers.

The Emperor of Delhi accepted his abdication and as a mark of honour and dignity, awarded him the absolute ownership of the Pargana (as a Zamindar land owner) and gave him the title of Dewan of the Pargana (Royal Revenue collector, Chief Treasury Official). The dynasty of Syed Nasir Uddin remained the Dewan of the Realm which was made permanent by Lord Cornwallis, the Governor General of India by an Act of Parliament known as the Permanent Settlement Act 1793 along with others like Chowdhurys, Amirs, Malik, and other prestigious people.

The Haveli (Indo-Arab residence) of a Ruler covering the vast area of land in Gothic design from one end to the other magnifying the glory of a Kingsly relic. Although destroyed and demolished after more than seven hundred years ago, people still speak highly of the Pre-Mughal era of India. The history Teacher Mr Saleh Sikander told us a brief story of such an era that existed at that time.

When we reached Lashkarpur, we found the fishermen had arrived with fishing nets and boats inside the wide pond. They started fishing enormous fishes from the huge pond, excavated during the Khilji rule in India. Syed Mahmud Hussain, a Judge in Dhaka High Court, a descendant of Syed Nair Uddin Siphasala was visiting home. He sponsored our school trip.

The picnic party was held by the huge pond in the nearby field where the soldiers assembled to receive orders and military technique from the General. The Judge himself shared the delicious food with us. It was not only a feast to enjoy, but a history of a dynasty and glory of the past we shared.

The picnic party ended with an exciting event. A horse race competition between the three Pargonas of Habiganj!

The villagers of the area starting coming in, we were surprised to see the great excitement of the local people. Ten horses participated in the race, organised by Dewan Syed Yaqub-ur Reza, the Dewan of Lashkarpur Haveli. I had no idea at the time, that this was my wife's grandfather!

Prizes were distributed to the winners by his son, Dewan Syed Shahid-ur Reza who was a Chief Justice in Dhaka High Court and would later become my father in law in 1965.

As a lover of race horses I really enjoyed this event which I remember til today, it was indeed one of the joyous occasions of my life. To think I was with my would-be in laws and I did not even know it at the time!

STUNG BY BEES

On one weekend, my brother Tutu and myself were playing a friendly game of football with our neighbours. There was a big playing field on one side, on the other side there was a deep bush inside the jungle. Our ball fell into the deep bush where there were many trees and shrubs mainly mango trees, blackberries and lychee fruits and unknown shrubs. We did not know that there was a big beehive on a bunch of a lychee tree. Our football dropped on the hive and all of a sudden a swarm of bees charged towards us. My brother and myself were the ones to get into the bush to find the ball. It was as if we were inside the bee hive, the bees surrounded us.

Our faces, eyes, hands and legs were plastered with bees. We screamed and screamed, but that did not stop them stinging us. We started wiping and sweeping them off our bodies and moving our limbs like we were dancing in pain but the pain remained as it was. We rushed home and had some herbal lotion applied all over the body. I had a fever and pain all over. After about three days it started to calm down. My sister's husband went back to the place, he covered himself to protect from the stings and then smashed the beehive to take the honey out. He brought it back home for us to eat. Fresh organic honey on the same day. Surprisingly it did not make me scared of bees but I do try and avoid them as much as possible!

MUHARRAM

According to the Islamic calendar, there are twelve months in a year. Each month commences with the visibility of the new moon. Muharram is the first month of the year, a very important month. Many incidents took place in this month of which the followings may be noted.

- Prophet Joseph was rescued from a well
- Prophet Moses crossed the River Nile whilst Pharaoh and the soldiers drowned.
- Prophet Jonah extricated from the belly of a huge whale.
- King Abraha attacked the Kaa'ba (House of God in Mecca – which was pre-Islam) to loot the gold and treasures stored there. He attacked with Soldiers and Elephants called 'The Year of the Elephants'. Abraha's soldiers were killed by stoning them to death.
- The most important incident in history was the Martyrdom of Imam Hussain (a.s) who was slaughtered by Yazid the Umayyad ruler. Referred to as the Battle of Karbala.

It was 28 November 1949, I was attending a procession in Longla, in Prithim Pasha State in the district of Sylhet, (Prithim Pasha was the Palace of Nawab Ali Amjad Khan) where the Shehen Shah of Iran visited for a tour.

It was 10th Muharram, the Day of Ashura and a solemn day of mourning. The date when the Grandson Imam Hussain (a.s) of the Prophet Muhammed (SAW), the son of Fatima-Zahra (a.s) and Imam Ali (a.s), was killed brutally and dismembered by the army of Yazid, son of Muwayyah in Karbala, Iraq. He was killed because he

61

refused to accept suzerainty of Yazid and wanted to establish justice from brutality. The shrine of Imam Hussain (a.s) is visited by many Muslims today. The holy month of Murraham and in particular the Day of Ashura is observed by Muslims in every country in the world.

Thousands of people cry 'Ya Hussain' and hold banners in the procession, they hold majlis and listen to lectures about history and the martyrdom of the beloved Imam.

Although Imam Hussain (a.s) knew the consequences as he had only a few family members with him and some friends, in total only seventy people. He had no intention to fight the huge forces of Yazid, but had no choice. the woman and children had been denied even basic drinking water. They killed them mercilessly, threw arrows into the children's necks and beheaded Hussain (a.s) Even after his death, his family were dragged into Yazid's court to be punished. His little daughter died when they brough his head to her on a platter in her prison cell. People curse Yazid and his army today and will continue to curse him as long as the world exists.

Mahatma Ghandi said *'I learned from Hussain how to achieve Victory whilst being oppressed'* and he also said:

'If India wants to be a successful country - it must follow the footsteps of Imam Hussain'.

Whilst I was a teenager, I thought of Imam Hussain (a.s). How he fought knowing that he would lose the battle of Karbala but with the courage and strength and self-sacrifice to empower us all. He was a seventh century revolutionary leader who made a stand for social justice and was the beloved grandson of the Prophet Muhammad (SAW).

Muslims all over the world hold a procession on 10th day of Muharrum to mourn the Day of Ashura and the martyrdom of Imam Hussain (a.s). If he did not fight for establishing justice, the concept of justice itself would have faded away from the surface of the World.

GET AWAY FROM MY COCONUTS

My Uncle was transferred to Dinajpur, a district in North Bengal and I had to travel there.

I did not want to go back to my Uncle's house, for fear of his strict rule and call for order. I remember whilst going to Dinajpur, my Mother gave me some money which she hid in a secret trouser pocket so that the pick pockets would not take the money from me. I was taken to Fenchuganj railway station with an escort. The train was approaching towards the station but before it had stopped, I felt a serious type of giddiness. I fainted on the platform! The train had left, and I was brought back home by the escort. I stayed with my mother and was feeling much better the next day.

I had to go by train from Fenchuganj for Akhaura railway junctions. At six o clock in the morning with the packed food provided by my mother and sister for lunch. I had to wait for ten hours on the platform floor. The trains were not so frequent as they are today, I had to wait for the train coming from Chittaganj to Mymenshingh through Akhaura.

It was so congested. When the train arrived it was already overcrowded with passengers. It was very hazardous journey on my own and very difficult to get onto the train as it was so overcrowded. Hundreds of people were waiting for the arrival of the train. I hardly managed a place to sit on. The train had arrived in Mymensingh after four hours. I had to catch another train to Bahadhurabad, a moveable station by the bank of the great river Jumuna.

I was just lucky to find a little space to sit on, but there came a big, tall man with a huge moustache and had said to me

"Hey you, move away from there! You are a little boy, you don't need the space, you can manage the journey standing somewhere".

I moved and was standing on my feet for some time. I became tired, I sat on the floor on the top of a bunch of a coconut bundle. But the owner of the coconuts started shouting at me.

"Get away from my coconuts!" I was helpless, nobody would show any sympathy towards me. People were so selfish and heartless.

The train stopped, I went out to relax a little, but the train started moving slowly and I had to get back on it. I got on holding the door handle and had to remain standing outside the train. I had to pass my journey with such a risk. It was night time but I was still holding the handle of the train hanging on standing outside the train. It was so risky and dangerous; I could have fallen asleep and fallen from the moving train but God helped me. It had become dawn by the time I arrived at the moveable station built on the sand by the river Jumuna. The station had to move its place because of flood. The ferry ship was awaiting by the river for passengers. The porters jumped on the moving train like reckless animals, looking for the luggage to carry. They were ready to take suitcases and luggage on the tops of their heads.

It was a long way to walk from the train to the ferry ship, it was so crowded and hard but I had the risk of my life. I was not suffocated and thankfully I survived. I had a place to sit on at least. There were too many passengers, the ship crossed the river Jumuna, it took almost three hours. The distance was not very long, but the flow of the river was so demanding, the ship was taken through the current and had to row itself against the tide to reach its destination. After crossing the river, when we finally reached the shore it looked almost like a mountain of sand.

The Wardens of many hotels started shouting *"Here is East Bengal Hotel"*.

Another said *"Bramania Hotel!"* pulling their customers in.

"Come and eat delicious food with meat, fish, Dhall and vegetable dishes, enjoy your meals with a variety of dishes".

The calls were going on in the air by the bank of Jumuna. This side of the bank was called *'Tistamukh Ghat'* meaning 'The Mouth of the River Tista'.

Two and a half hours later, after the rest break, the train was loaded and started with a slow speed due to the sand of the river banks. However I was not looking forward to the fact that I would have to change the train again. It reached Parbatipur, another railway junction and had two hours left to reach for Dinajpur. I can never forget such a horrid experience of my boyhood. It was a two day and one night journey in total. I finally arrived at Dinajpur where my Uncle was living.

DINAJPUR

I was admitted in Zilla (Government) School, Dinajpur. My Uncle had me joined to Mukti Fouj Cadet Group. We had our own uniform designed by the Fouj group. It was a white shirt with a badge on the shoulder, white socks with white canvas shoes and a green cap with a moon and star on it. It was really smart looking and charming. We used to get together every week on Friday afternoons in a sports ground as schools were closed on Fridays. After usual instructions of discipline, obedience, responsibilities, patriotism and many others. We used to go on the parade with national songs and bands. We chanted

"Pakistanir quomi fouz, Amra paharadhar chora bazaarer shaitan dol hushiar, hushiar.....""

Meaning we are Pakistan's national cadets, we protect and safeguard our country from any aggression, beware beware! I had to play drums and trumpet in the band. The roads were not so crowded with pedestrians, carts and rickshaws and haulage carriers. Finishing the parade and march we returned to the base. After that there were instructions again from our leaders to *'love thy neighbour'*, good citizenship, human rights and responsibilities, helping each other and many more. We finished the program before the darkness approached.

THE TUTOR

In Dinajpur we had a private tutor at home, engaged by my Uncle to teach my brother and myself. We were taught Mathematics which we were very weak in. I was the eldest brother and needed more help in Maths. After a few days the teacher changed his attitude, he became so arrogant. He started hitting and beating me when I could not produce the right answers in Maths. The practice of his hitting increased. One day I thought it was a bit too much, it must be stopped!

My brother and myself complained to my Uncle, but he shouted back at us! He said it was unmannerly and disrespectful to complain against a tutor and that we should behave well with him as he was a Teacher. I was helpless. One day he was beating my brother Tutu really hard with a bamboo cane. I could not tolerate it anymore. I lost my temper and *shouted at him, saying,*

"You should not beat him like that! He is not an animal!" I took a deep breath and continued with a heaving chest,

"If you carry on hitting us like this you would find the consequences!".

I snatched the cane from his hand and broke it into pieces and threw it outside into the garden. my Uncle heard me shouting at the Teacher, he found a long datta (a sort of long vegetable stick) and started hitting me for being insolent and aggressive towards the Teacher. The Teacher was smiling at this. In those days the Teacher's used to beat their students and we had to tolerate this.

He even said to my Uncle,

"When the boy grows up, he will turn out to be a ruffian or a gangster".

My brother and I wanted to leave and join the army to save ourselves. Every year when the army recruitment bureau came, we would appear as candidates for recruitment.

The Army recruitment Bureau came to Dinajpur and recruit boys and adults to the Army. I would have been a perfect candidate for these posts however in the interview I was always asked would my guardian give me permission to join? I used to say there wont be any problem with me getting the permission. Then they asked, who was your guardian, I would

say the name of my Uncle. At that time they refused to take me on, they used to say come back to the recruitment centre when you have graduated and we will consider you in the Commission rank, and you can find a choiceable military career.

WEDDING IN CHITTAGANJ

I was living with my parents at home during my school holidays. I had to go to Chittagang with a cousin of mine, representing my Father and family. The wedding took place in a luxurious hall. It was a wedding quite unique of its kind. My cousin had been a Captain in the army. He was working as Divisional Manager of Standard Vaccum Oil Company. The bridal party arrived in a well decorated wedding boat, through the river Meghna. The Hall had a huge reception area, fitted with a vast counter on which various kinds of fresh fruit and juices were displayed. on the other side there were a few tables joined together with special food for the wedding but there was no table service! The guests were supposed to take the food on their plates themselves according to their own choice.

Some of the guests started whispering saying "They did everything so nicely but could not afford the seating arrangements for the guests or tables to have a proper dinner!" It was a shame. Musical was playing whilst guests were standing having dinner, talking, joking and having fun. At the end we returned to Sylhet, to our home where my father was eagerly waiting to hear about the wedding.

We recanted the evening back to him. He wasn't surprised at all, and smiled. He told us it was a modern trend to have a buffet dinner and explained this meant eating while walking and talking. It our country people were not yet used to this system and did not understand it yet. That is why some guests were shocked and whispered to each other.

They had expected the traditional sit-down dinner which prevailed in the Indian subcontinent at the time.

THE COURTS

Back at Dinajpur, our school used to have a 45 minute lunch break. The school was situated in a place whereby there were many amusements of different kinds. My brother and myself used to enjoy them all. There was a monkey dancing, small circuses, tight rope walkers, singing and dancing in the street, toys and handmade music equipment for children. The hawkers sold many products of interest to children on the fields near the open market.

On the other side where the college, the Police Station, the Judges and Magistrates Courts, I found a lot of interest in the affairs of the Magistrates Court. The court affairs, the trials, arguments, etc. I enjoyed them all but had to depart to attend my classes at school.

When I was a student in College I used to accompany my father attending Court. He had court cases especially on land matters. I assumed I might have to deal with these matters one day as I was the eldest son of a landowner.

TRAINING

Due to the division of India both Hindus and Muslims were tense. Some apprehended of reoccurrence of disturbance between the two countries sooner or later. Compulsory military training for civil servants, people from schools and colleges and statutory and non statutory organisations was introduced.

We students also had to join such training. It was simply a defence tactic but involved some advanced level training for adults. There were organisations like Girl's Guides, they had to undertake their training under officer ranking female soldiers. The University Officers Training Corps (UOTC) had to undergo such training to defend the country from foreign aggression. Youths finishing the training could join the regular forces if they wanted to. I was a trainee myself, under the East Bengal Rifles as it was called in 1950.

THE RETREAT

In Dinajpur we were living in a big isolated bungalow which was originally the residence of Dr Peter Osborne the ex-Head of Church in Dinajpur, North Bengal, during the British rule in India.

After his departure back to England, the house was acquisitioned by the Government and renamed as the official residence of the Senior Deputy Commissioner (my Uncle). The beautiful eight bedroomed estate was surrounded by a mango tree garden. It had lychee trees, jackfruit trees and a Gulab Jaman (White Plum) tree and many others. We were so fortunate to have so many fruit trees within the boundary of our home. We enjoyed the fruit to the core of our heart. Everyday before going to school we used to climb up the lychee tree and ate as many lychees as we could.

We used to ask each other,

"How many did you eat?" Some would say fifty, some would say 80! But we had to also eat breakfast too before going school!

The school started at 10 o'clock but we had to reach before as we had to attend the assembly whereby the Bible, Quran and Geeta used to be recited by the respective religious teachers with translation. The attendance used to be registered there after which a simple exercise lesson was provided then the class would start.

The big detached bungalow had an annex attached to the main building. It was called *'The Retreat'*.

We five cousins and a teacher used to live there. The building had four bedrooms, it was situated towards the mango garden. There was also a guest house, and the guards and servant's quarters. Nearby was a garage for five to six cars. There was a tube well shed; when the tube well was pumped, the water used to be stored over the roof of the house for distribution wherever necessary including the kitchen, bathrooms, dining rooms and in a separate washroom for common use.

The most horrible part was in the Annex where we used to live. When we were in bed; we used to see with our own eyes, that a huge monster like body covered with black hair all over sitting on our bed and breathing aloud! Or someone was walking with shoes or sandals in the room. The next morning, we found all our shoes scattered!

We ignored the strange happenings for the first few weeks but how long could we ignore such a regular occurrence and spend nights with our eyes held open with fear? We had to rearrange our shoes and sandals scattered all over the floor. Besides at night every moment a mango from the tree used to drop loudly on our tin-covered roof making an offensive noise! At least two of us used to go out to find the dropped mango and take it, otherwise the squirrels would grab them. We had to be quicker than the sly creature!

Whilst we could not forget about the ghost affairs, it would need to be stopped as soon as possible. It could not go on like this! We had to mention this to our religious priest who used to teach us Arabic. He was also experiencing this phenomenon as he slept in the other room, but he did not mention it otherwise it would have become a big concern for everyone in the house. He said he tried everything in his capacity but could not get rid of the phenomenon. He reluctantly advised us to inform my Uncle and see what he says about it. My Uncle and the family were living in the main building and they did not feel anything at all.

I was chosen by the group, including the Mulla (Priest) to bring this matter to my Uncle. When I spoke to him about it, he became stern and asked me:

"How could a man and ghost live together? I don't believe it"

On one night I saw him walking along alone with a stick surrounding our side of the building with a torch in his hand. I thought it must be my Uncle, nobody else would walk at this hour of the night. I was observing him and I started wondering how come he was walking alone with a stick around the house. I started watching through the ventilator over the wall. I called the Mulla and I counted it. It was three times that my Uncle went around the building. It was midnight, he did exactly the same thing again. There was no appearance of the so-called ghost in the room. We slept in peace that night, we lived almost three years in that house undisturbed. My Uncle must have scared it off!

ILLNESS

In the District of Dinajpur, Malaria was a common disease. At least one of us fell ill with the disease, at least once or twice a year.

During the period of illness, my Uncle did not allow us to eat normal food. We could eat only the recommended plain food that was allowed. One day I became so hungry, I could not bear it any longer. I said to my bother Tutu who also stayed in Habiganj with me in my Uncle's house. I was so hungry that I felt like going to a restaurant and eating rice and curry.

Tutu said *"What! are you joking, you have a high temperature how can you walk to a restaurant?"*

I said *"My willpower would lead me there"* and we started walking although I was very weak.

It was an ordinary restaurant for ordinary people covered with a bamboo mat only. We had only a small amount of money with us, that was all.

I asked the Manager *"What have you got?"*

He said "We *only have Beef Curry, Pumpkin Bhaji, Dhaal and rice"*.

I said *"Bring these dishes please for the two of us"* and we both ate and filled our stomachs. Although the food was of cheap quality we ate to our heart's content. I being the patient started feeling much better.

Walking back home, on the way we noticed a tractor with a long trailer full of sugar cane heading towards the sugar factory at Shetabganj. Some kids were running behind the tractor for the sugar cane. The people on the tractor threw a bundle of sugar canes towards them. They took the full bundle themselves and gave us a few canes. We took them to the sports centre by the playing fields and happily started cracking and breaking the sticks to suck the juice out of the sugar cane. I was feeling very salubrious on my way home!

I had no temperature, no illness and was feeling quite fit. I felt that I had recovered completely. My aunt then started serving me normal food for dinner and I was much obliged. Thank God I was cured!

FITKIRI

I remember an astonishing story which was directly connected with me.

We had a very good cook who could cook nice Indian, English and French dishes for prestigious foreign people living in India. Nowadays you can take prestigious people to 5* Restaurants to entertain them however back in those days it was a disgrace to do so. You should entertain them at your residence with home cooked food by your chef.

It was Abdul, our cook who said to me that he was getting lazy and forgetting how to cook foreign dishes and that he was getting old day by day. I told him that he could practice cooking those dishes even today if he wanted, and to start with a small dish. For a joke I said that my aunt had saved some eggs from English hens that we had. My aunt had saved those eggs for breeding purposes. I told him to use those to cook a dish to start with. He said that it was a great idea and he would do so.

We went to the place where the hen was sitting on top of the eggs, we took all the eggs from my Aunt's saving pot and he cooked a special French dish and some other dishes as well. It took some time but we did not have the patience to wait for the food to be cooked. It was after midnight. We were awake and awaiting to taste his practice dish. We devoured the food and it was delicious.

The next day my Aunt noticed that all the eggs were gone! She wondered how did it happen as they were kept safe and well cared for.

She was astounded at their disappearance. She thought it must have been the act of one of the maidservants, our favourite. Her name was *'Fitkiri'* whose habit was to steal edible things or any special food cooked at home. Her eyes must have fallen on the eggs. My Aunt asked her, threatening and shouting as if she had taken them.

She denied and said she had not. In fact she did not steal the British eggs! My Aunt became so angry, she called the 'Chaprasi' (Orderly) of my Uncle and had sent for an expensive candlestick to put it alight by the side of a grave of one of the Indian Saints (Pir Sahib) who was dead. He was well respected by the ordinary people who believed that the Pir Sahib although buried, would take action against the wrong doer.

As a result Fitkiri, the poor girl had severe diahorrea which was completely unrelated but everyone started blaming her for telling lies. My Aunt kept telling her to admit that she had stolen the eggs and she would be saved from the punishment.

We knew that it had been us! they were blaming her for nothing. We were the culprits! I kept on telling my Aunt that it was not her who stole the eggs. It was us. Why should she suffer the punishment when she is innocent! But still nobody would believe that it was us because Fitkiri has the habit of stealing food even from a boiling pot!

Sometimes she would have the food in her mouth and say she had not eaten it. But this time it really wasn't her! Sometimes the innocent one is punished and the real culprit is released. I felt so bad about this.

BETA

Myself and my brother loved going to the open market in the centre of the town in Dinajpur. My Aunt usually sent our domestic worker Amir to get the daily shopping. Tutu and I accompanied him one day. We both noticed there was a price difference in the commodities but the quality was the same!

I called Amir and said "T*his Betta (unknown man in Sylheti language) is selling vegetables at a higher price when the same things are being sold at a cheaper rate at other stalls. How come there is such a difference?*" before finishing my sentence, that same man came out with a stick and was about to hit me!

He said, "*Why did you call me Beta? Can't you see I am so much older than you, nearly over sixty years old*", he exclaimed. "*Do I look like your son? You are just a kid born yesterday. How dare you call me Betta? I won't spare you!*" by saying so he raised his stick to hit me.

Amir quickly stopped him and told him we were from Sylhet and we address unknown men by calling them '*Betta*'. He shouted, "*Do you know who he is?*" he continued, "*He is the nephew of the Senior Deputy Commissioner, if you hit him, you will be arrested!*". By this time a Police constable had arrived and the man moved away, scared.

Bengali people do not use the word Betta, only Sylheti people use this term. There are many words Sylheti's use which Bengali's do not. While in India and Pakistan people address Betta to a younger person or child in a loving manner, definitely not to an old, unknown person.

BACK AT FENCHUGANJ

During the Christmas Holidays I came back home to live with my parents as usual. In the winter months the tigers came out to the villages at night to search for their prey. They used to drag out the cows, calves, goats and sheep, from the sheds and kill them. Sometimes they attack lone human beings or give them a severe fright! Some experts go to the jungles to look for these tigers during the day time. They go into the jungles where the tigers had been seen or located.

I asked my father if I could go and join the fun. I had never seen the tiger hunting before. He allowed me to go there but sent two guards along with me to the jungle. There were so many people gathered together there to see. The professional hunters knew where to find the tigers, they built a fence or barrier surrounding a big area and gradually reigned this in to make it smaller and narrower like the walls closing in until the tiger became trapped with nowhere to go.

The tiger would start jumping and roaring as a ferocious mighty animal. Some people started running away out of fear while hundred dared to remain to watch the entrapment. The Ronigarh which is a small and narrow area. This is the most enjoyable part of the game. The tiger angrily and out of fear, takes its bigger teeth out and starts jumping and roaring. The trained people hit the tiger with large spears which angered the tiger even more, but it could not do anything, as it was trapped. The people could shoot the tiger but they wouldn't do that. That would have to be permitted by the owners of the land where the tiger was trapped for killing. Once the land owner or his representative permits, the people could have the permission to through the arrows at the tiger intending to kill it. This was if the tiger had killed their animals and was dangerous to the community.

The tiger took his big teeth out and hissed at the people. It looked like it was about to pounce on someone. The trained professionals had to use their arrows and spears to put the animal down and kill it. The tiger would then be taken first to show the family of the land owners, then taken to show the hunters family.

This was the age-old tradition of tiger hunting. Its fur was displayed in the hunter's house or used for a luxurious rug. It was a great accomplishment

in those days, to kill or tame a tiger who was known as the King of the Jungle. This practice was widely used in the rural areas of Bangladesh where there were hills, forests and mountains.

BANANA STORY

We had a long garden with different kinds of bananas by the four sides of our pond. My father had them planted as a hobby, the pond had a boat sunk under the water for fishing purposes. Our domestic workers used to float the boat to the surface of the water and dry it to catch different kinds of fish or for boating trips.

We used to sell bunches of bananas to wholesalers, who used to come to the canal by boat near to our pond. The men used to check the banana trees and counted the bunches. They noticed that a bunch of the special kind of bananas were missing.

My father got angry and in the public gallery he said "*This sort of incident has never happened before in my boundary, nobody ever dared to commit such an act. If I ever find out, who did it, I will deal with them myself with a stern hand*".

People maintained silence and no one said a word. A few days after he found these bananas are being distributed for iftar (breaking the fast) during Ramadhan.

My father said, "*They looked like those bananas which were stolen!*"

The Imam who led the prayer in the mosque said, "*We were the ones who took the bananas, they were special bananas we wanted to distribute them for iftar so everybody could eat them!*"

We were so surprised, and could not stop laughing about this. Later on, it was revealed that I had been involved in the plot. Stealing the bananas to feed hungry people just like Robin Hood!

GAZIPUR

One day myself and my cousin Mona Bhai decided to go to my Fufu's (my father's eldest sister) house in Ghazipur some six miles away from our home. On the way we brought two bags full of fresh fruit from the market at Fenchuganj. When we reached the sugar cane fields, all of a sudden there came a group of monkeys which surrounded us!

We had to stop in our tracks out of fear. The monkeys came straight up to us and snatched our shipping bags! We were so surprised and shocked we did not know what to say. There was no other shop around to replace the fruit we bought for our Fufu so we went to the house empty handed.

They were surprised to see us unexpectedly. We had to tell the sad story to them, but they were not surprised at all! They said this was a norm and a regular occurrence in this area which happened all the time. The local monkeys were so mischievous, they got up to all sorts! Shopping bags are snatched away, even food from people's hands and they ran away giggling into the distance. You can't help but laugh yourself! We all fell about laughing about this. What fun! We had a nice meal that day, made quickly to entertain us. We enjoyed the food and had some rest for a couple of hours before returning home safely.

NILPHAMARI

In 1951 we came to Nilphamari, a sub-division of Ranjpur District. My Uncle had been transferred there as a Sub divisional Officer (SDO) responsible for all statutory departments in the subdivision. I was admitted to Nilphamari Govt. High School. My closest friend was the nephew of the sub divisional Superintendent of the Police.

We used to stick together at school, during the class time or playing, cycling or going on school trips. I was a bit hot-tempered and ruthless sometimes. My friend Adil's Uncle the Police Super Intendent did not like my attitude in case his nephew adopts tempestuous habits from me.

He asked Adil not to associate with me, who came to school and told me this. As we were very close friends, we could not stay away from each other. He said he would show his uncle that he had no connection with me, but this was not long lasting. Sadly, he left Nilphamari for good, as his Uncle had a transfer order for Mymensingh another district. I became lonely again.

ARMY RECRUITMENT

Whilst in Nilphamri, we noticed that Army recruitment was taking place. My brother Tutu went to the recruitment centre to try and get recruited by the army, away from the control of my uncle. He was recruited as a Cadet in Electrical and Mechanical Engineering.

He was taken to Chittaganj army camp to be sent by ship to West Pakistan. When my uncle came to know of this, he sent a telegram to my father to take him back, but that was not possible as the ship had already sailed for West Pakistan!

After a few months Tutu wrote to me to say he was having a very hard time. there was no time to relax there as everything was under discipline. He joined in the army to avoid the strict rule of my uncle and avoid studies, but he had to follower an even stricter regime and regularly attend his studies, parade and learn military practice. It was even harder than before!

At this time after Tutu had left, I felt so incredibly lonely and very unstable. I had no hope or aspiration to live. I felt so lonely. The only friend I had left me because of the sudden transfer of his Uncle. I felt more of a burden in life when separated from my friend especially on the weekends and I missed my brother immensely.

I went to join 'The Ansar Force' a Paramilitary Corps Camp like the National Guard. I went to the camp intending to join. I was recruited for training only on weekends. That was only to spend the time, not intentionally to join the force as a career. The Adjutant found me quite sanguine. He wanted me to join the regular force later on, after my matriculation exam. After three months of weekend training, I completed the course and was told that they might require me on a state of emergency only. I agreed and signed for it.

I started going hunting mostly on my own. I had access to my Uncle's shot gun which was not being used. I asked my Auntie if I could use it and she permitted. I was not sure if my Uncle knew of this but I had been using it on a regular basis. Sometimes I used to shoot three of four birds, sometimes I used to return home empty handed. It gave me pleasure and I really enjoyed hunting., At times I started thinking very seriously about my life. I had no hope and no ambition in life. I missed my family so much, and felt so much emotional pain. I could not bear it any longer and wanted to die. I was coming home late every evening for the past few days.

My Uncle started shouting at me so arrogantly saying that he had been telling me not to be late so many times and I should not be coming back after dark in the evenings. I was a bit careless, I thought he would not be home at this hour. Normally he would be late coming back home from office and I would get away with coming home late. On that day he was very angry with someone and started shouting at me.

He said "Go away from my house, if you do not listen to me".

I became angry too and went away from in front of him and was sitting down on the edge of a Well.

He was having his dinner and had a chicken leg on his plate and said to my Auntie,

"Why did you give me this chicken piece, go and give this to the Son of the Big Boss". (He used to call me this when he was angry)

87

He took it to one side and told my Auntie to give it to (Khuka) me. I heard him saying this as the Well was not far from the dining room. I started thinking that this was my Uncle who had told me to go away from his house. This was the same Uncle who kept the chicken leg for me! He must have really cared for me. The same Uncle who had stayed on my bedside all night when I was sick from seeing the Ghost and who took me to Royal Military Hospital in Shilong when I was ill. I realised that he loved me so much, he was just angry that's all.

I came back to my room to sleep, I began thinking to myself. 'Why would I go away from him? He is so kind and caring. If I leave, I would remain just a villager! No! I would not run away. I thought to myself, why should I feel sorry for myself? God has created me with a purpose. If I took my own life I would be answerable to him. If I had to suffer, I would suffer. God who gave me life it is only for Him to take it away. No, I would not take away my life away whimsically. I would live, I would struggle, I would bear the pain and sufferings of life like a badge of honour. I would struggle for my existence and achieve the best I can in life. In fact I got back the strength, the stamina, the hope and aspirations which I had lost in that moment.

THAT ASSAMI BOY

During my time at High School in Nilphamari and attending school, my class mates used to look to me differently than other students. They did not accept me easily. I used to look somewhat different to them and also could not speak with their colloquial accent. I would speak plain Bengali with a Sylheti accent, but it was different to the way they spoke. Therefore I could hardly make any friends there. As I came from Sylhet, they called me 'Assami'. They always used to address me as *'that Assami boy'*. In the classroom, any naughty things which happened were mostly blamed on me! Even when asked by the teacher, they always pointed as me as the culprit. *'He did it! That Assami boy'*. Before India was divided in 1947, Sylhet region was in the Assam province. I felt saddened by their attitude and sometimes lonely and lost in the school due to being singled out as different.

One day in the playground they were blaming me for some wrongdoing which I did not do. My class friends not only blamed me but shouted at me with a loud voice. I told them to stop it and that I did not do it. They started teasing me in a way that I lost my temper.

I grabbed one by the neck and had said *"If you carry on blaming me for what I did not do, then I will break your neck!"*

The Games teacher then intervened. He asked me what was happening, I said it was just an argument nothing else. The teacher said he does not wish to see any mishap here. He went away and after a few mins and that boy said *"I will teach you a lesson"*.

And I grabbed his neck again and said "*I'll teach you NOW!*" I started to slap him repeatedly. He was quite frightened at my attitude.

I said "*Never ever bother to think of taking revenge or else you will remember that Assami Boy forever*". The boy was the Ring leader of the team, and after this incident, no one approached me again to make any trouble.

THE LANGUAGE MOVEMENT

It was 1952 when The Language Movement started. The Government of Pakistan was about to introduce Urdu as the state language of Pakistan. The East Pakistani people (now Bangladeshi) who were the majority in East Pakistan took to the streets in protest against this as they would lose their mother tongue of Bengali.

They demanded that Bengali should be one of the State languages of Pakistan alongside with Urdu. But the Government completely ignored their demands. The Government would not listen and installed Urdu as the ONLY national language of Pakistan. This was very difficult for East Pakistanis who had been reading, writing and speaking Bengali all their lives. Demonstrations took place everywhere. The middle class, working class, students, children, shop owners, everyone came to the streets to protest, even the Government Servants and the workers from the factories went on strike against the government's decision.

The people of East Pakistan, known later as Bangladeshis started the language movement nationwide. Many people and enlightened students of Dhaka University namely Salam, Barkat, Rafique, Jabbar and many more lost their lives when they were shot to death by the Government on 21 February 1952.

It became a remarkable day in the history of Bangladesh known as EKUSHER FEBRUARY when Bengalis demanded their national language to be recognised by the nation. The day is remembered every year. I myself joined in the protests and believed in the cause.

Due to the mass demonstration, schools had been closed for an indefinite period. I was thinking to myself, that this was not a solution to the problem. We would lose our education this way as there was no end to it. The schools were closed for indefinite period. So I took a handful of friends who were students and found a few teachers that were still available. I insisted they come to the classroom and teach the few students who were still eager to attend school.

We tackled the strike and started going to school. The Student Union leader and their followers got angry with me. The leader named Kalam came with a bike and threatened to break my teeth if I continued to do this.

I replied that until all my teeth are broken, I would attend school! I would like to see the brave, daring person who could do this to me! Seeing my courage and determination, he took his sandal from his feet and gave it to me to hit him with! I looked at him and he apologised to me and said sorry. He said I should slap him on the cheek with his own shoe for his threatening behaviour! I joined them in protest some of the days and attended school the other days because I believed in the cause, to protect our mother tongue of Bengali.

When the strike was over and normal school resumed its sessions, I noticed that no one sat on my side of the row of benches, it was all empty. The students did not even sit near me. The teacher came and asked why one row was full and the other only had one person, me. The students replied that they were boycotting me and did not want anything to do with me.

I laughed out loud and said *'Yes it is me, King of the Realm, nobody has the audacity to sit beside me'.* After a short while, they accepted me back into the fold and collectively voted for me as Captain of the Class. They saw my determination and ability to lead the students for a good cause and looked up to me with inspiration.

DREAMS

I used to suffer from horrible dreams throughout my childhood. No matter where I stayed and in what condition, I believe my loneliness, helplessness and bitterness of life caused my bad dreams. One of which I always remember vividly was that I saw the whole world had been destroyed. Everyone was rushing towards a tunnel to save their lives. There was only one way to get through towards the tunnel.

It was so busy, there were thousands of people waiting in the queue. At the end of the queue there was a big tall man who appeared like a black giant. As ugly as he could be standing at the end of the tunnel with a big shining sword in his hand.

When the people approached him, he grabbed their necks and beheaded them one by one and threw their heads to the wild ocean behind him without even looking where he was throwing them. People out of fear of such a brutal act started screaming.

It was now my turn. He extended his long hand towards me to grab my neck and do exactly the same as he did to the others. I woke up screaming out of fear with a loud voice, my family members rushed to see what was going on. They found me in bed shaking.

I told them of my dream but they consoled me in different ways. They thought it was an illusion. I did not understand the significance of my dream yet, it might have been the effect of the hopelessness and depression of my young life.

THE NAWAB OF BENGAL

As a student in High school in Nilphamari, I was chosen by the Sports and Drama teacher to play the main role in a Drama called 'Nawab Sirajud Daulah'. The Nawab of Bengal, Bihar and Orissa in India at the fight with the British in the battle of Plassay in 1757.

The story involved Mirza Muhammad Siraj ud-Daulah, commonly known as Siraj ud-Daulah, who was the last independent Nawab of Bengal. The end of his reign marked the start of British East India Company rule over Bengal and later almost all of India.

He was betrayed by his Commander in Chief Mir Jaffar Ali Khan who accepted a huge sum of money as a bribe from Clive of East India Company who promised him the governorship of Bengal if he did not put of a fight against the British in the battle of Plassey.

The Commander, Mir Jaffar Ali Khan in lieu of the bribe being a big sum of money, he accepted the offer and betrayed the Nawab. He did not fight against the British in the Battle of Plassey. The Nawab was defeated, he was caught while fleeing away by a boat and was killed with the order of Clive. Robert Clive was a Seaman when he joined East India Sea Company. Robert Clive then took over the rulership of Bengal and the administration of India. He became the first Governor General of India. A new rule of the British India emerged and he became Lord Robert Clive, Governor General of India.

One after another, Governor Generals were elected by the British Parliament as the Governor General of India. The British ruled India for one hundred and ninety years until 1947. Lord Mountbatten was the last Governor

General of India, the Uncle of Queen Victoria of England and Empress of India.

An international film has also been made about the Nawab Sirajud Daulah. I played the part of the Nawab, I was so proud to get this main part after auditions. All the parents and staff attending the show really enjoyed the performance and I became so popular at school after this. I became the Captain of Nilphamari High School after this.

CINEMA

Whilst in Nilphamari I started going to the cinema on a regular basis but without the knowledge of the elders. The cinema hall was just on the other side of the football ground. The owner of the hall used to come to my Uncle to obtain permission for exhibit the films. In those days the Chief Officer, called the Sub divisional Magistrate had to provide a written permission called a 'No Objection Certificate' to exhibit the film. The films supposed to be viewed by adults only in those days.

The owner used to invite me to the cinema, mentioning the name of the new film. The Sub divisional Magistrate and his wife had two special chairs reserved in the hall. It was a tradition since the British era to reserve two seats for the SDM and his wife. But my Uncle and Aunt did not watch films in the cinema therefore their seats remained vacant. I was the only viewer from the family to go and watch the movies so I used to sit on their chairs. It was only me who took advantage of this special tradition.

I was actually not allowed to watch the films but after dinner I used to escape from home and go and watch all the new films! I would have to go in a split process and watch an hour a night to complete the film without anyone noticing. I did not want to get caught by my Uncle, and the Owner of the Cinema hall did not mention it. I asked Habib our servant, not to tell anyone about it.

I watched a lot of Indian films this way as I was a naughty boy at that time!

RANGPUR

In the year 1953 my uncle was transferred to Rangpur from Nilphamari. I was admitted into Class nine, a year before the Matriculation (GCSE) in Rangpur Govt High School. As usual I was weak in Maths. My Uncle engaged a private tutor for me only to teach me Maths. My teacher was very efficient and very busy too. I had to attend his home every evening, he had two other students from the school. A few weeks after starting lessons with him, I was progressing better in preparation for the exam and my teacher was very happy thinking that I would do better in the final exam.

My teacher was newly married, he used to go to the living room to see his wife frequently. We had a few minutes to relax when he went out of the room. Opposite the house there was a girl who was learning music, singing loudly with Asian musical instruments which caused a distraction to us. We complained to the tutor but he did not act. I thought that we had to do something about it ourselves.

When the tutor went to see his wife the next time, we at once went to the house opposite whilst she was singing, we banged loudly on her front door and then returned to our lesson. We had been doing this for a few days as the tutor did not do anything to stop the nuisance. One day her father noticed that it was us banging on the door, the students from the house opposite. He complained to the tutor who then shouted at us. It was Durga Pooja time, when the Hindus prepare for prayers, we decided to organise a music event in the evening. We knew that the neighbours would participate in the event along with the family of the girl who played music.

We asked the neighbours who were mostly Hindus, they were so excited. They took the lead. Many singers and music lovers from our neighbours were invited. We did not have to do much. We took the initiative and the neighbours did everything. Luckily at that time the girl from in front of our tutor's house had completed a full course of music lessons and was about to receive a final certificate.

She had to sing a song with the musical instrument in the presence of the neighbours and friends, the music lovers.

After a few days we heard that she became engaged with a music teacher and got married to him in another town and thus we thankfully got rid of her!

TRAGEDY

With a heavy heart I have to mention an unexpected incident that took place in our school in Rangpur. It was the day of our annual prize giving ceremony, it was supposed to be a day of joy. But it ended to be the most painful day for us. There were many distinguished guests including the District Commissioner, District Judge, the Principal of Carmichael College and parents where also present. The prize giving ceremony took place every year, students were given prizes for competitions at the end of the event.

The people present were all greatly happy. At the end of the programme, refreshments of various kinds were distributed with cold drinks. Our Headmaster who obtained a master's degree from the UK, was speaking jubilantly to the guests, eating some sandwiches. All of a sudden he choked, stopped eating his face turned blue and his airways blocked. He collapsed in a heap on the floor. The guests became shocked and one of them had a chauffeur driven car who took him to the hospital immediately as an ambulance service would not get there on time.

The doctors in the hospital tried their best in every possible way to save his life, but they were unable to revive him. It was such an unfortunate event, a sad end of our beloved head master. Mr Rouf. We missed him immensely after this loss. I remember what happened, whenever I eat a piece of sandwich. He was such a popular and respected head master who was loved by all and lost his life unexpectedly at the age of only fifty two years old.

INTO MEDICAL SCHOOL

In the year 1954 I passed the final matriculation examination for the East Bengal Secondary Education Board with a good division. I wanted to be a Doctor, I wanted to help the poor and destitute to have no access to normal health care services.

I applied to Sylhet Medical School. I was interviewed and accepted to study medicine in that school. The name of the course was L.M.F (Licentiate of Medical Faculties) a four year course and a one year practical training as a Doctor in the emergency services. After that one could study a year more for a condensed degree leading to M.B.B.S, or one could practice as a qualified medication practitioner or obtain a job in public service as a Doctor. In the first year of the L.M.F Course, in additional to medical studies I had to study the science subjects in Sylhet Government College, only because I wanted to stay close to my parents.

I remember one of my relatives used to be an executive civil servant, he came to know of my exam results when he came to our house. I said I submitted the exam paper earlier than three hours had passed in the exam hall. As I did not do well, I came home early. He said to my uncle,

"I knew he could not do very well, he will never amount to anything!" I heard him talk about me in a condescending way.

When my results finally came, this relative was astounded that I passed and I had been admitted to study medicine. He was so shocked he said

"How could he have gained entrance to medicine?". He had no comprehension that I could achieve this and was completely shocked.

100

Later on in 1967, at some time I went back to Bangladesh from the UK. This same relative invited me along with other guests to have a feast. He introduced me as his nephew Kuka, he lives in England. He had three restaurants there and had earned good reputation in the catering industry.

They all shook my hand and congratulated me for achieving such a success. I was that type of boy who was once a lonely youth, useless, good for nothing 'goon' said by some!

TICKET PLEASE

Whist in Sylhet I used to live in the medical hostel called Alamgir Medical Lodge, whilst a student in medical school. My parental home was only 15 miles away and I used to come home almost every Thursday or Friday to spend the weekend with my family by train and return on Sunday night or early Monday morning.

One day, I was a bit late, I could not reach the station when the train was waiting to depart. I got on to the running train which was moving at a very slow speed. When it was getting on to the railway bridge which was of a higher level I got on as it slowed down. The door of the train was left open for more wind to blow inside the compartment as it was too hot. There was no room to sit on, I was a standing passenger along with many people. All of a sudden I noticed that a TTE (Train Ticket Examiner) from the special branch put his uniform jacket on encrusted with an official badge.

He approached towards me and asked, '*Ticket please*'

I said '*Sorry I could not buy a ticket, I just got on to the train. I had no chance to buy a ticket. You must have noticed that I climbed the running train before the bridge*'.

He did not want to listen to anything and again asked '*Ticket please*'. As I was unable to produce a ticket, he booked me for travelling without a ticket.

He told me, '*There is a mobile court on this train. You are going to be charged for travelling on the train without a ticket*'.

He told me that I will have to appear before a court headed by a magistrate and I will be sent to jail if I do not pay the penalty. The full cost of the ticket would be forty-eight

102

rupees for travel from where the train was originally coming from Narayanganj and a penalty.

I told him I had only one rupee which is the correct fare from Fenchuganj to Sylhet. He told me, there is no excuse and that will not do. In that case I would have to appear before the magistrate and he would send you to jail. I requested him to let me go, I am a student. I have no more money with me. I appeared before the magistrate who listened to me. He allowed me two hours to pay the full train fare as charged by the TTE including the fine a total of forty eight rupees. It was ridiculous as my correct fare should have been less than one rupee for the short journey I travelled, but they made me pay the whole amount from the train's own commencement journey.

At first I went to a relatives house and found them sitting on the veranda having tea. This was the relatives who always used to be welcomed to my home and fed lovely meals but even though they knew I lived in a student hostel, they never asked me to come and eat at their house. I asked for a loan and they told me they didn't have any money at the moment, so I left. I had a wristwatch I sold it for 50 rupees to a watch maker. I got the money and paid the mobile court and was released. It was a sad incident. I had no intention to deceive but I had to pay the penalty regardless. I lost my beloved wrist watch which I could not replace it easily.

THE HOWER

In late summer 1955, a severe flood engulfed the lower part of Sylhet district. A team of medical students and doctors were sent to Sunamganj by my college on a large boat in aid of the terrible disease cholera, diarrhoea and small pox. We were sent to remote villages in Sunamganj area to perform vaccinations. We started with eight members in our team, we took our boat through a big hower (big natural lake) to reach to our targeted villages. The hower was so big and wide, one could not see the other end. It was just water and water, nothing else was visible at all. There was water spread all around us and it was overflowing. The houses from a distance looked like they were floating in water. People were living in distress, there was no clean water, no food, the lives of the people were threatened with severe diseases. We were to give initial advice and preventative medicine and vaccinations. We started sailing through the hower to reach people.

On one Saturday after lunch, we met together at the medical compound and started out again as a team. We started at 2pm but we reached the hower when darkness fell over the whole area. The two boatmen with us used to row the boat in howers they knew. They kept on rowing the boat for such a long time. We saw the lights on the other side of the hower, we used them as a guide to reach the destination. The first targeted village. Some of us were dozing, some were sleeping and the boatmen were busy rowing all night.

It was morning, the sun was out and we were surprised to see we stayed exactly in the same place we started from! We could not believe this! At the end we reached the village in the afternoon when we should have been there at dawn. He was been rowing all night in illusion but had stayed in the same place. Once we told the villagers, they were not at all surprised. They told it is happened sometimes, it still remained a mystery to us. Some might say we did not move anywhere, or we rowed in a circle and returned to the same place, or indeed the boat had been held there by a ghost! We will never know.

It really did happen, it was not a fairy tale.

MISCONDUCT

In the second year of studies, I had to complete a presentation of the organs of the human body. I had to appear for a verbal test leading to intermediate L.M.F. I was in my Anatomy lesson and was in the middle of my demonstration and we were having an oral test on paper cards showing different organs. I was demonstrating the oesophagus or the gullet and the card was in my hand.

Halfway through my demonstration I forgot the correct word and stumbled. My anatomy teacher grabbed my card and threw it on the floor.

He shouted at me '*Did you come here for a joke?*' I picked the card back up and replied

'*Why are you treating me like a primary school student?, How could you throw my card on the floor like that? What that a joke?*'

He became very angry and reported me to the Head of Anatomy. The Head called me in for disciplinary action and warned if I ever behave like this with a Teacher he would make my life miserable and would never give me a pass as long as he stayed Head of the Anatomy Department.

I replied '*I do not want a pass! I am leaving for good, I don't want to study medicine at all!*'

By this time the incident was reported to the Superintendent of the Medical School who without making any inquiries of his own, imposed me with Severe Warning, a huge financial penalty of ten taka and notified my class of my 'Misconduct'. He also served a Notice to the classrooms.

I was so upset and agitated at this injustice. I rushed into the Superintendent's Chamber and accused him of misusing his position of power. I didn't not even ask if I could enter his room. I was a very short tempered young boy and if something feels wrong to me, my blood just boils. I just could not accept when people do not act in a fair and just manner. He did not even bother to ask me about the incident without taking this action.

I rushed into his room and told him arrogantly,

'You did not bother to ask me what it was about, just served the notice of misconduct with a fine. I am not paying a penny of this fine as a penalty. I am leaving the studies of medicine for good'.

I came out of his room straight to the dissection hall. I packed my books and instruments, I took my gown off and came out of the school angrily. I withdrew from the entire course, rushed to the halls of residence and sold all my books and my skeleton set to the first year students and took the late train home.

My father asked me what happened at my sudden arrival so late at home.

I told him the whole story in anger and that I have given up my career in medicine. He showed me a letter that had come from the faculty of medicine before all this happened. It stated that I would not be allowed to take the final intermediate examination as it had been revealed by the examination board that I was two months short of age to sit the exam under the current regulations, due to my birth date being in August!

This letter came all of a sudden and it was a shock to me and my father. My place would be removed from the register and I had to wait another year to take the exam. I asked my father about this and he believed it to be the fault of the Medical Board who had scrutinised my candidacy and decided this.

They should have identified or informed me of this when starting the course, he wanted to take legal action against them for the compensation of the loss of time and tuition fees when they have accepted me onto a course which I cannot complete. I said to my father there is no need to fight this case, as I have already left. He asked me what would you do now, in the middle of the year?

MOVING ON

I knew my father was worried and I reassured him I would get into another course and complete my degree whatever happened. I read in the newspaper that the admission date for Carmichael College in Rangpur had been extended due to the floods. It was a well known college, many of the civil servants were ex-students from Carmichael College. I said to my father I would be leaving home tomorrow to enrol.

So I started accordingly for Rangpur the next day, it took me twenty one hours to reach the college due to severe floods at that time. I finally reached there and decided to move into arts subjects instead of medicine, it was 1956. On the same day of my admission, I began the first year of an Arts Degree Course. It was a four-year degree course, two years intermediate and two years for the Degree. The very first lecture was in Economics. I noticed the teacher was walking and talking and a student shouted with a loud voice,

'You better go back to the podium or we won't listen to your lecture' . The lecturer however carried on speaking.

The student then jumped over the desks and pointed his finger towards the lecturer.

'Didn't you hear what I said?' He shouted at the lecturer.

It was a class of over two hundred students. Nobody knew me at this college so I stood up, as I could not stand back and watch this. I raised my voice at the student and told him not to behave in this way. I told him to behave like a gentleman and respect the educational facility. I told him to maintain the order of the college without causing any problem. He seemed to sit down after that.

At the recess hour the Principal's orderly asked me to go to the Principal's office and he had sent for me to see him in his office. I was thinking to myself, *'Oh no not again! It was only my first day'.*

To my surprise the Economics teacher was sitting in one chair and the Principal in another.

He said *'I wanted to say thank you for the way you dealt with the situation to bring the class into order'.*

I told him it was my first day in this college. I got the courage to continue on and did not care that I left the career in medicine. I realised now that it did not suit me. After two years I passed the intermediate exam. During this time I lived back with my Uncle in Rangpur. I became known to the other students in the class as a ruthless student in the college.

I met quite a few students whom I knew in school life in Government High School Nilphamari and Ranjpur Government High School. I missed two years studying medicine and some of my other friends missed one or two years and we all met at Carmichael College in Ranjpur. I became likeable and popular in this college. I was nominated as the Assistant General Secretary of the College and in the next election I was elected the Assistant General Secretary. The student member was more than eight thousand. It was my usual habit to go hunting everyday and a friend of mine from college joined me.

I found the Arts to be so much easier than medicine and found myself thoroughly enjoying the classes. I used to study seven to eight hours a day excluding the regular classes while in medical school but in Arts I did not need to study much and I found it so easy. I had five subjects to study, English, Bengali, Economics, General History and Political Science at intermediate level.

OUT WITH THE PRINCIPAL

The college had a large number of undisciplined students, it seat of multi-political groups. The students were engaged in demonstrating against any political issue against the government or something in the college. I remember when I became a student in the college. Principal Asghar Ali, MA, a Barrister at law from London, was transferred to another college of repute and a new principal took over. His name was professor Salman Chowdhury. He was extremely strict, rude and unfriendly. He thought, he would bring the students under his strict rule of law and order. That did not happen and the students revolted against him. Police were called in due to riots. Some of the students were arrested, they were taken to the police station for questioning. As a result, all the students raised their voice with a big rally and started a demonstration against the principal. It was a big chaos, they raised their voices, shouting out

"Principal, leave Rangpur!" and so on.

There were thousands of students demonstrating against the principal. They shouted so loudly,

"There is no place for Salman in Rangpur!" the college was sealed off by the police to maintain peace and order. The district commissioner ordered the police to disperse the mob. The police was chasing the students and arrested some hooligans. The rest of the students were running towards the railway bridge, over the canals and behind the bushes, wherever they could. I also stated running! I had a cycle bought a few days before, I hid under a bush. If I was caught or arrested by the police, my uncle the Additional District Commissioner would not spare me! It would be a disgrace if I were arrested. I was hiding by the canal under a bush and came back home

111

before my uncle arrived home. I was wet with dirty water and had changed all my clothes before he returned.

The Principal was escorted by the police with the order of the commissioner to Fulcherry ghat, the ferry station to get into the ferry ship to cross over the river Jumuna into another district Mymensingh and his life was saved from dishonour.

BLACK GHOST

It was a strict order of my uncle to be back at home before evening time. One day I was really late arriving home. He was very angry and was loitering and pacing up and down from the end of the veranda to the other. I could not hide myself and he found me. He scolded me quite loudly in front of my two cousin sisters and their friends. It was really embarrassing for me, they were laughing and giggling at this and started teasing me with a funny face. I vowed to myself to take revenge! I knew that they were scared of ghosts from when we heard a story from an old next door lady.

We had a detached small building on one side of our home. It was a Pooja house, a Hindus worshiping temple which had been vacant for quite some time. We did not go near to the idols and no one ever bothered to enter the temple except for the daring rats and mice. This was originally build by a Hindu zamindar who built and owned the temple. I decided to make use of the building, at least for once.

I got into the building, dressed myself up in a black burka and covered my whole head and face with a black scarf. Wearing a black pair of knee length boots on my feet, I came out of the Temple. There was a loud cracking noise when I opened its door as it had not been opened for a long time. It was just before midnight, I was not scared at all and instead was plotting my revenge on my cousins!

When I saw my cousin sister Hamida was going to the kitchen, I approached towards her pretending to grab her. She was scared to death! She screamed aloud!

Everybody came out of the house, my uncle and aunt came out too. They all found a black ghost roaring and advancing towards Hamida. My uncle reached into his room, picked up his gun and came out to the scene ferociously. I got scared at this, I was thinking this would be the end of my life, if I did not jump into the well! I thought my life is more valuable than the false ghost. I unveiled myself to save my life. Everyone saw that it was only me, not a real ghost. I had to confess that I dressed up as a ghost to frighten my cousin sisters for laughing at me the other day when I came home late. It was a real tit for tat. My uncle probably knew it was me all the time. It was such a funny story!

STUDENT MARRIAGE

There was a notable incident which took place whilst I was a student whereby a student from Rangpur Govt. High Girls School fell deeply in love with a second year degree student. It was going for some time but there was a time when it was exposed and we all had concern for the girls family. The girl's father was very influential and powerful landowner named Mahtab Chowdhury of Nilphamari district of Rangpur division (north Bengal) who had the title of 'Khan Bahadur' awarded by the British Government long before the Indian independence. He was very cruel, ruthless and whimsical.

His daughter was living in the school hostel in Rangpur where security was of vital concern. When this was known to the school authority, she was expelled from the school and also from the hostel. When her father came to know about it, he was furious. He came to Rangpur from Nilphamari with four of his men and armed bodyguards. The Chief of the Police and others from respective departments were also present. He summoned the guardian of the boy (who happened to be a brother of the detective police inspector) for questioning. Whilst they were doing this, the students of the College got together in the Circuit House.

The Bride, and the Groom was already present. The students announced the marriage. They had already summoned a priest and in front of all the student guests the marriage was solemnised, and myself, the Assistant General Secretary of the College acted as guardian of the bride. The father of the bride, was too late! He came in a rush, but by that time the marriage ceremony had already been performed and solemnised.

We, the students put the newly couple in a hired taxi and placed a just 'married sign' which slowly approached towards the groom's house. All the students not less than a thousand paraded behind the taxi in a gorgeous style.

The traffic on the road was standstill. The most powerful father of the bride had nothing to say when he saw so many supporters greeted and congratulated the newly married couple for a long and happy conjugal life. He came to the groom's house with his men where he was honourably welcomed as father of the bride.

THE MYSTERIOUS FOX

On one night I was sitting in my room. I saw that some old aged female neighbours came to me with a complaint against a fox. How interesting. I asked them what the problem was.

They said *"It was a ferocious fox"*.

I replied, *"Still better than a cruel human being"*.

When I asked, what was the complain about. One of their spokesmen said to me,

'*We can't go to the well to draw water. When we go near the well, the fox frightens us with a roaring voice and drives us away from the boundary of the well. We heard that you help people. Do you know that the young people nowadays just laugh and pass us by without helping'*. They were really upset. The well had been in a dark place and no one wanted to go there.

The house nearby had a lantern fuelled with Kerosene Oil. The area was not lightened enough by the lamp. However they said to me, I should go along and see for myself. I went to have a look at their request and found a fox was standing like a guard by the well. When it saw me it started roaring angrily at me. I came back and took a double barrelled shot gun, this particular gun belonged to the Maharaja of Samara which my Uncle had bought from a public Auction.

I used to use this gun for hunting. I hid the gun behind my back and was still holding it. The fox was standing like a statue. When I approached a little forward he started to growl. The women, out of fear standing at the shadow of another house and been watching fearfully.

I shot at the fox with the double-barrelled gun. It came running towards me furiously, still roaring but this time with a different howl. It showed me its big teeth in such a manner that even I started shaking. Did you ever see a fox with its two spikey teeth out, roaring like as a ferocious animal? It looked to me like it was not a fox but a Cheetah.

It started running towards me, so I shot at its chest but it would not stop.

I ran from it to save myself from the fury of such a dangerous animal. But I came to a dead end of a building, finding no other way, I hit it hard with the gun. The power of the animal was so much that the impact on its body broke my gun into two pieces. Only the barrel remained in my hand. I hit it again with it to save my life. I thought that it was the end of my life, standing before me. Suddenly it fell to the ground, it's two teeth still protruding outwards. It began bleeding a stream of blood.

A lot of people came out of their homes including the women who had left me alone to fight with the ferocious animal. The neighbours were surprised to see such a huge fox almost like a royal Bengal tiger.

STUDENT TRIP

I was enlisted for a trip as one of the students to visit the Maharaja's Palace in Mahiganj. We were going for a picnic party by the side of the Palace. We were sixty students altogether both male and females. We started the journey at Nine 'O' Clock in the morning from the college there were no coaches available in those days. Our Professor Abu Hena Mohammed Mohsin, head of the department of political science. He had arranged three trucks for the trip to the Palace in Mahiganj. We took Chefs, Cooks and Kitchen Porters and a lot of cooking pots and pans and all necessary cooking equipment including rice and spices. It was not a sandwich affair! When we were passing through the built up roads with the load exciting music from the microphones in the well decorated trucks, the people came out to the streets so excited and asked who we were and where we were going. Someone said that we were the students of Carmichael College in Rangpur going to the Mahiganj Palace for a picnic.

When we arrived at our destination, the uniformed guards at the Palace greeted us with Honour as if we were esteemed guests of the Maharaja. We went to park our vehicles in the car park near to the six banks of the pond with looked like a natural lake. Nearby was the Palace of the Maharaja. The women of the Palace used to have a bath in that lake in the evenings which is why it was so isolated.

The Maharaja engaged some fishermen with a huge net who started fishing as arranged by our College so that we could enjoy the fun when big fish started jumping and flying from one place to the other. Oh! it was so much fun, so nice and enjoyable. Words cannot describe the beauty of the flying fish before us. The fishermen had to used two boat already docked in the water to spread the net over the lake. Only the huge fish were kept and the others were thrown back into the water. At that time, the members of the Maharaj's family came out to participate in our lovely picnic. They spoke to us and were very friendly. Some of us were very interested to talk to them about their past life and so on. They would happily talk to us and were pleased to be having fun. By this time the big fish had been caught and were being cooked on site. We were called in to watch our chefs and cooks, the cook from the Palace also came out and joined in to help cook the food.

We then started a tour of the Palace as arranged. We also visited the stables, the park, the swimming pool and grounds of the Palace. The whole area was covered with high walls, built in approximately 1680 which special thin bricks for the Maharajas. There were annexes built for other purposes. By that time the food was cooked in four items of different dishes. The family of the Maharaja joined us to have the meal in the outside grassed area without any dining table and chairs. We ate on grass together like a family as it was a picnic. We enjoyed the site, the flying fish, the food and the company of the Maharaja. The Professor was so excited, he asked the students

'Lagche Kemon? (How is the food? Are you enjoying the food?)' to all the students. He was in a happy mood, as were we all. We all exclaimed 'Besh Besh (Excellent)' Raising our hands upwards and nodding our heads.

Our picnic trip was very enjoyable for everyone. The Professor had liaised with the Maharaja's Dewan and had arranged the great party. The Maharaja system had been abolished by the Land Acquisition Act 1947 but were still respected as part of the golden days of the past. The Maharajas, Dewans and Chowdhurys are still respected today.

THE CREMATORIUM

One day while returning home by cycle alone from hunting, I was passing through a road by the Crematorium in the deep darkness in the late evening. There were rows of trees on both sides of the roads. Suddenly I noticed that a black monster spreading his legs on the trees on both sides of the road, standing. I looked again and again and saw the same image before my eyes. I was stunned at the sight!

Frightened, and terrified so much that my whole body went rigid and started trembling and my heartbeat quickened. I had no option whatsoever but had to continue and pass through between the long spreaded legs of the black thing. On coming back home I felt shaky and giddiness and did not know what was going on with me.

My Uncle was walking alone on the Veranda awaiting my return. He saw me going straight to my bedroom and he thought that this was abnormal for me. I lay down in the bed and he came to me and asked what was wrong. He touched my forehead and found I had a high temperature. He called the doctor in a hurry who came and treated me with some tablets. My Uncle stayed with me all night by my bedside.

I did not have anything to eat that day but after midnight I felt very hungry as I did not have lunch or any snacks because I went from college straight to hunting. The night had passed, my Aunt was also very concerned of my condition. the next day she cooked a special dish for me with rice and shingi (a fish available only in the Indian subcontinent) which was very light and not too spicy. I had only a little and I did not speak much, I went back to sleep again. My Uncle thought I has an illusion of some kind. He recited some verses form the Holy Book and blew on my face and chest. This worked wonders. From the next day onwards I started to feel normal again.

ON THE RICKSHAW HOME

In Rangpur I spent joyous days of my young life. The people loved me so much although I was a Sylheti, I could speak their language, their dialect, quite well.

They used to say 'Khoka hamar Ompurer sawa bahey', meaning Khoka is a son of Rangpur!

Unfortunately my uncle was transferred again and I went home to stay with my parents. I was very sad when he was transferred to Sylhet before his retirement.

I went home to study for my intermediate test examinations. I did not have the money to go back to Ranjpur. I saw one of my Uncle's in Fenchuganj who was a Police Super intendent, he was on annual leave.

He said 'Hey You, What are you doing at home? You should be in College?'

I told him I need money for the train fare to get back to Ranjpur. He immediately put his hand in his pocket and gave me some money to pay for my living expenses in Rangpur. At the same time his brother also came to Fenchuganj, he was an Engineer. He gave me an open return pass to get to Rangur which is to be used as a train ticket. How lucky!

When I went back to take the exams, I found it difficult as my uncle was not living there anymore. I used to stay at my friend houses sometimes, but they were also students, and we could not afford proper meals sometimes.

One day one of my distant relatives saw me in a rickshaw. He stopped it and took me to his house, he was an ex-major in the army and was living with his small family nearby. He later became a Central Labour Inspector.

Thanks to him, I had a place to stay and regular meals. I passed the intermediate test exam but I did not have any money to pay the fees for the final exam or for my train ride home.

EXAMS IN BOGRA

I decided to go to Bogra where one of my cousins was working as an Engineer with a government department (Communications and Building). I did not have any money. I only had a sack of a few clothes, some shoes and a watch given by my younger brother who was a trainee military Engineer.

I decided to pawn my watch to pay my exam fees. This was the second time I had to do this! But it did not work as the watchmaker thought I was trying to sell a stolen watch and refused to take it.

Luckily, a brother of one of my friend's who knew me from school age saw me and asked me to go with him. He took me to another watch makers and helped me sell the watch. The very next day I paid the exam fees but didn't have any money left over, even to buy a snack or to make the journey to Bogra.

I completed the exam and passed the Intermediate Exam (IA). With a few annas (coins) in my pocket, I bought a stick of chewing gum to curb my hunger. I then mustered up the courage to get on the train without a ticket and waited anxiously as the ticket collectors entered the train from the back. Luckily there were two of them and engaged in talking to each other, they forgot to ask for my ticket. When the train stopped at my destination I got out and eyed up the two exits gates. I chose the gate that was the busiest and started yelling 'stop, wait' as if I was following a porter who was carrying my luggage. I managed to sneak through!

I called a rikshaw without any money in my pocket to pay for the fare and thought I would deal with that later. The rickshaw brought me to my relatives house and I found

125

my young cousin and asked if he had any money. He reached into his pocket and luckily had enough to pay the rickshaw driver. I got inside the home and was greeted by warmth and comfort of a family home. I chose a lovely bedroom settled myself there. My eldest cousin brother was so happy to see me as if he had found a great friend in me.

THE JOB

A few days later arrived another Engineer, this time an Executive Engineer who was transferred to Bogra (which became a Division of C & B). He quite liked me and asked about my circumstances. I said that I had heard of him and I knew his brother Adnan from Government High School. He was very surprised and asked how I knew him. I told him I have moved around with my Uncle Mr Munawar H Chowdhury who was the District Magistrate. He was so pleased to meet me and we had a great time having a chat and some tea together.

He told me he had been posted here without any administrative support and asked if I could help him as his assistant. I told him I was not qualified in this field but I could give it a go and I would be pleased to do so. Taking on a new adventure was my kind of thing. I was appointed as his assistant working on the same desk.

The contractors, officers from the district collector's office and all related persons assumed I was an Assistant Engineer which I was not. I worked from 8am until around 9 or 10pm and put my every effort into the job. My cousin thought that this would be the end of my studies, but I assured him that I would definitely complete my studies.

THE BOSS

While in Bogra there was an outbreak of small pox and a lot of people were attacked by the disease. The government then circulated an Order to the public to refrain from eating certain meat foods. For about seven months we did not have any meat whatsoever, only vegetable meals. The butcher shops were closed, the owners were suffering financially. It because impossible for them to survive in business at that time.

After the period was over, the situation became much better but it took around seven to eight months to clear but I remember the time was very hard on the local community.

Myself and my cousin used to walk together a lot especially in the evenings. One day we were going to Ramadhan prayer at night, some people followed me, thinking that I was the Boss and that I could provide jobs for people. This is because I was working at the Divisional Engineer's office.

There were jobs in Construction, building roads, brick manufacturing and many others. As I was quite a healthy lad and my cousin, was a very thin man, the people mistook me for the Sub Divisional Engineer of the department on many occasions! They saw me sitting down in the office with the Chief Divisional Engineer, in fact I was newly appointed only as an administrative helper to him.

My cousin used to address me as 'Boss' jokingly, because I worked at the head office. When I was approached in the street for a job, I used to tell people to come to the office and we would try and help them.

My cousin used to say jokingly, 'You should not walk with me. I spent a lot of my time in obtaining my degree in engineering and now it looks like it was for nothing!, You did not do your degree and you are addressed as 'Sir' and asked for jobs!' he continued to say I wonder why people believe it and respect you as a boss' He laughed.

I used to reply as sarcastically, that it was not my fault, I looked like a boss!

HEAD INJURY

While employed in the Communication and Building department for the government of Pakistan I had to go and visit a building site with the Chief Engineer in Santahar, about thirty five miles away from Bogra town. We went in a Land Rover driven by a driver of the Company, an ex-army personnel. On finishing the job we were coming back to Bogra through the highway.

All of a sudden there came a Morris Minor car, driven by a young man from a side road coming to join the highway. It came in front of our vehicle and we could not avoid it. We had a serious accident that day. Our car had some damage on the front, and the other car was almost smashed on the front. We had an emergency stop. Suddenly appeared a military vehicle who witnessed the whole affair. They took us all into the nearby general hospital in Santahar. The driver was seriously injured. There was blood all over him. His face was completely damaged, his jaw was broken and he had lacerations on his face.

I had a slight head injury. After initial treatment I was released home, and started attending office after a few days following this terrible shock.

DON'T SLEEP

I was working so hard at the office whilst being a student. It was very difficult for me to work at 8am until 10pm after studying all night. I used to sleep covering my body with a cotton sheet so that I would feel cold and my sleep would break early in the morning and I could prepare for my lessons. After this I would have a shower and breakfast and go to work.

After coming home from work at night I used to have another shower to stay awake, had my dinner with my cousin and returned to my studies. At this time I felt so tired and exhausted. When some more staff joined the office I was able to leave for a few days to take my final exams. I had to transfer my exam centre to Bogra and came out successful in the Intermediate final exam in Arts.

After I passed the intermediate final exam in arts, my cousin gave me a treat to visit the palace of the Nawab of Bogra. Nawab Muhammad Ali was the Prime Minister of Pakistan in 1953.

ELDER BROTHER

One day I received a letter from my father that my two younger brothers Jitu and Bachu were going astray. They were not paying attention to their studies and were spending too much time hanging around with boys from the village. They used to be engaged mostly with angling, cycling, fishing and playing football. Even at the time when they were supposed to be studying, they were enjoying themselves outside.

My father asked me to leave my job, go home and motivate my brothers to study well. I agreed to go home and motivate them to study so I looked for local jobs close to home. My presence was a little scary to my younger brothers. They started to listen to me, sitting down to study and concentrated harder on their homework. I used to sit with them like a tutor and teach them. When their school came out, I was pleased to see their progress.

At that time, one of my cousin brothers Jalal Uddin joined them. I started teaching all three boys together. My brother Bachu had a good memory and I gave him extra coaching to take an active part in school activities.

At the next prize giving ceremony, he won first prize for reciting poetry superbly! We used to have a lot of appreciation for students who learned to speak well on stage, whether reading aloud or reciting poems or stories in a good voice and with vigour. It was highly celebrated in Bangladesh.

GOOD FOR NOTHING

I remember when one of our naughty cows was eating and damaging our runner beans and plants. I shouted for domestic workers to come and tie it up with a rope. My cousin brother who was a railway guard on the express train, after finishing his night shift he came home tired and was resting. He told me, I shout not be shouting for the domestic worker, and I should go and tie up the cow myself!

The cow was covered with mud and the rope was covered in cow dung. I did not want to touch it! The cow damaged the plants because it was roaming freely. My cousin said I was good for nothing because I did not stop the cow.

In our village there were many bridges made of bamboo, it was not like today's bridge. People used to cross the canal through the bamboo laid down as a pathway for crossing. I was also waiting to cross the bridge while I found a ten year old boy who was standing on the bridge about to cross the canal. The string bridge started wobbling, it was dangerous, he may have fallen into the water flowing under the bridge. A man walking at a distance was shouting

"Save him! Save him!"

I took the risk to go to him and save him from the wobbly bridge by holding him hard so he wouldn't fall. A few moments later, my cousin brother who had called me good for nothing, saw me. He could not believe his eyes!

HUNTING FISH

I was very fond of Alwa Shikar which was the hunting of fish by a specially made weapon with a wooden stick fixed with many metal spikes. I used to go with my cousins to do this type of fishing which was so much fun. U usually went on a dark and quiet night. We could only hear the howl of the foxes from a distance.

The lake was not too far from the river Khushiara where the fish came from. We had long torch lights and held a kerosene lantern. We used the torch lights to focus on the fish before we plunged the spiked stick into the water. Sometimes we did not manage to catch any fish and other times we were very lucky, but it was all good fun! On our return home, we used to spread the fish on the dry floor on our front yard. In the morning everybody woke up and were so surprised to the fish were still alive and jumping looking for water.

Sometimes I used to go out alone to row a boat on the river alone, rowing slowly in the amber light of the sun to revive the spirit of my life.

VICTORIA COLLEGE

In Bangladesh, during the summer months, the quilts had to be folded in and stored away in the cupboard until the wintertime. It was extremely humid during the daytime but cold at dawn. I used to unpack the bundle of quilts and fold them back neatly. My cousins always knew who was the best person to take the quilts out and fold them back so nicely. It was me!

My family would say, it must have been Khoka. He knew that I was preparing to go to England. He used to say "I don't know how Khoka will live in the cold weather of England!"

When I did move to England in the future, when my cousin heard that I was going to open a restaurant he was most surprised as he thought I could not run a business without ever having been to the bazaar in my life! He thought I would be sitting on the till as a lazy man, not doing anything!

SYLHET MC COLLEGE

I travelled to Dhaka, the capital of East Pakistan looking for work. I was not able to secure a government job as I was not mature enough as they were considering people over the government recommended age.

I became despondent and was going back home empty handed. This is when I met my father's cousin who was the Superintendent of the India/Pakistan Border Police. He had a family and two sons and was living far away from them. He took me under his wing and helped me to enrol in Victoria College in Comilla in the first year of BA Degree. He wanted me to stay with him as an adult member in the family and not to run after jobs but to continue my studies to become a university graduate and obtain better jobs. But I was continued to look for a full time job with full intent to complete my degree through evening classes. But that didn't happen. I was not that lucky. It ended in failure. I could not find a full time job at that time.

But I longed to go back home and go to MC College in Sylhet so that I could go home and look after my brothers during the weekends.

After a lot of deliberation I secured a place in MC College so that I could complete the final two years of my Bachelors in Arts.

LIAR

I was attending my history class at MC College, the name of Professor Hitti was mentioned by my class mates. A student in my class called Zubair, who had a habit of stammering whilst speaking pronounced the name of the professor as "Hi Hi Hi Hi Ti". The students used to make fun of him and call him that name when they saw him at college. Zubair got really angry and thought it was me who taught them to mock him, but it wasn't me! I wouldn't do anything like that. I was new student and he approached me to accuse me of mocking him. He threatened me for saying this. I told him I did not even know that he had a stammer, he kept accusing me and calling me a liar.

He threatened me "*You are a liar, I will make you admit it*" he said.

He had hit a student in the past, so bad that he had a bleeding nose outside the shop in front of the college gates. The students in the class told me to apologise to him to prevent any further issues. But I told them I had no reason to apologise as I had not done anything wrong, I told them, "*I am not that kind of a coward*".

I remained adamant I would not apologise. He came up to me with the fists raised to punch me in my face.

I said to him "*You don't know me. I have already been to two other colleges before this, I have deal with many of your kind in the past. I came here thinking that MC College would be my last stop. But I can see know that you will not let me do so. I ask you for the last time, not to raise your hand on me otherwise I would be so rough you would not imagine. You will suffer for good*". But he did not listen and punched me in my face!

I raised my hand saying, *"Ok take it. Now you will remember for the rest of your life"*.

I gave him an almighty punch, a blow that made him fall from the concrete steps down to the bottom, right in front of the student union building. All the students that were stationed by the stairs were talking and wondering what was going on. Nobody asked me anything. He was bleeding so badly but he did not complain to anyone.

He did apologise to me and said *"I am sorry, I thought you would be like the others. I did not realise that you were so tough!"*. At the end Zubair

became one of my very good friends at college. He thought that this friendship would strengthen him as more of a hero in the college.

I did not have any conveyance of my own and used to walk almost three miles to college and back each day. Zubair used to come to my house and pick me up on his bike and took me to and from college everyday. He because my closest friend until our graduation in 1960 when we obtained BA Degree from the university of Dhaka.

MONKEYS

While at home I used to go to my eldest sister's house as usual one or twice a day. Her house was about five minutes walk from ours. Most of the days I used to have lunch with her. Once I heard her children started shouting "Monkey! Monkey!" for they saw a monkey on a mango tree. They got scared and started screaming. I came out of the house and took the gun out to shoot it, but the monkey was really frightened. He looked at me like an orphan child, he folded his hands together as if he was begging for mercy. I felt so bad and sorry for him. I put the gun away.

This was the first time I ever saw that a monkey was craving for mercy like a human being. He was so cute and looked at me with two eyes and a sad mouth. I let him go free.

He raised his hands and clapped at me which made me smile. He was thanking me for leaving him alone and jumped with joy and sometimes used to come back and see us from afar, but he never came close again.

COCONUTS

Another day in the early hours of the morning, I was returning home from visiting our family graveyard. I was passing through the coconut trees and suddenly I found a naughty boy in the village trying to steal a bunch of coconuts from the top of the tree.

While putting the coconut bunch he accidently dropped it on the head of another boy who helping him steal the coconuts by waiting at the bottom of the tree. He started screaming!

I arrived on the scene at that time. The boy on top of the coconut tree, out of fear, lost his control and dropped to the ground right in front of me.

They immediately jumped up and ran away as fast as they could for fear of what I would do. They were running and shouting,

"Sorry Khoka Bhai! We will not do it again!" I laughed at them.

THE HOLDER OF THIS PASSPORT

When I completed my degree in 1960 I looked for jobs everywhere. My father's financial situation started to deteriorate, and I needed to secure a job urgently. The government had started acquiring lands and some of our lands were taken away. Some with compensation and some without.

Our Income was drastically reduced; my father had no regular income. With so many litigious actions and family commitments, he became quite exhausted. He did not want the community to find out that he was financially suffering. I, being the eldest son, thought it was about time I help my father in every possible way I could. Finding a well-paid job was quite impossible at that time, and even if I could find such a job, my salary would not meet my father's commitments at home.

I had an international passport obtained in 1958. My Uncle had made an application for me at the employment exchange to apply for a passport and the application to work in the UK. Britain needed people from the common wealth countries, as cheap labourers for employment in the thriving industries in the UK. I was quite surprised when the package came redirected by my father sent to Bogra during my final Intermediate exams containing my passport. When it arrived, I looked down at my passport which read *'The holder of this passport is proceeding to the United Kingdom for employment'.*

I was so pleased, but there was one huge problem. I did not have the money for the plane fare! I stayed impatiently in Bogra and finally when I came home I told my father about the passport.

I was excited and wanted to go to England for employment. I was the eldest son and had six younger brother and four sisters. We had a big family to support. Two of my sisters were married. I asked my father for permission to go to the UK. But my father vehemently objected.

My father did not want me to go to England and said,

'What job will you do there? You have no skills whatsoever for manual work! Will you be a labourer cleaning the factory floor or the roads, or cleaning public toilets? I will not allow you to do and do these sort of jobs. Surely you can find a better job here in Bangladesh!' He was completely against it. He would not allow me to travel to the UK to do these manual jobs.

I started looking for jobs in Bangladesh. I travelled to other districts and finally, I found employment with Pakistan International Airlines in their Sales Department at the Dhaka Head Office. The joining date of which was next month. I went around to wealthy relatives and friends asking for a loan to buy the ticket fare, without the knowledge of my father, but failed.

All of a sudden a distant Uncle of mine who was in the UK for long time working as a Engineer wrote a letter to my father suggesting him to send his adult son to the UK as many people who came were doing different kinds of jobs and there were many prospects out there.

After much deliberation and having read this letter, my father finally agreed to give me permission to go to the UK. I requested him to reply to this letter saying that he has a son who had graduated recently, and he already has a passport valid for travel to the UK. On receipt of this letter, my uncle, Mr Ashid Ali sent my plane fare!

Then was no stopping me! After all, my father had agreed on one condition, that I must further my education there.

But his Aunt, my Grandmother said *"How can you be so hard hearted to send your son so far away!"* she exclaimed, *"You wont see him very often, it would take five or six years to see him again!"*. But I was feeling positive, to go abroad instead of joining the job with Pakistan International Airlines.

MY JOURNEY

On 6th April 1960 I came to Dhaka to fly to England. The flight left Dhaka Airport towards Karachi en-route to Heathrow Airport. My father, my sister Anawara and her husband came to the airport to bid me farewell with a heavy heart. The plane left Dhaka airport and after about 15 minutes flight, the Captain announced that there was a mechanical fault on the plane! The aircraft wont be able to fly anymore. They asked permission from the Calcutta Aviation Authority to land at Dom Dom Airport in Calcutta owing to mechanical failure. Permission to land was refused because it was India.

The Captain then announced that we had to go back to Dhaka. It would be a hazardous journey to return to Dhaka and that it was very risky too.

We the passengers were panic stricken, worried and insecure about the journey back. We did not know what would befall us ahead. Would we be able to reach Dhaka this way? Some passengers in the flight started thinking that this might be the end of our lives. Some started to burst into tears, the aircraft crew were also very worried. There was a lot of chaos on the flight. They tried to cool down the situation and console the passengers as best they could.

By this time we arrived back to Dhaka Airport. We were dropped home by the coach of the airlines to our houses in Dhaka or the relatives houses from where we started from. I arrived at my sisters house, knocked on the door, they were in bed but awake. From outside I could hear them talking through the veranda. I heard that they were talking to each other about how I left without even looking back at them for the last time! It was quite ironic actually that I had come back again.

144

My sister heard a noise, it was me knocking on the door. She thought it could be a burglar outside and said to her husband, "*Who could it be? Who could knock on the door so loudly and repeatedly at this hour of night?*"

I thought that knocking the door this way would scare them so I started calling out her name and then her husband's name instead.

They then shouted out '*Who is it?*'.

I said '*Its me, Khoka*' (my nickname).

They heard my voice and opened the door. They were astonished and looked at me with wide eyes. I told them of the whole story with the airlines. We then came to the room where my father was sleeping. He came out and saw me back. My father was surprised at my sudden return within two hours but his eyes lit up at the chance to see me again.

He said '*This is good, we will go back home together to see your mother tomorrow!*'.

It was a ten hour journey by train which we both took the train the next day. When I got home, my Mother was so happy to see me back, rather than being worried. We got some extra time together by a stroke of luck!

After five days stay in Fenchuganj, I had a telegram calling me to go back to the Airport for a replacement flight.

STUCK IN KARACHI

I took the next plane out and when I finally landed in Karachi airport I had to stay four hours as a transit passenger to fly to Heathrow. I then found the Manager of Pakistan International Airlines standing there over the counter and talking, Oh no! I had left Dhaka without starting the job. Was he going to cause a problem for me while leaving the country? I was due to join his department in the Sales Office in Dhaka next month and I hadn't informed them of my departure. I was so afraid I ran to another side of the airport and tried to hide away.

Suddenly a policeman grabbed me and took me to his office in Airport Immigration and accused me of holding a forged passport. He would not believe me that I had a genuine passport obtained on proper application. I saw three other boys sitting down like me and the officer said,

'This is a forged passport how did you obtain it?'

I told him that I had obtained the passport after proper application and police verification. He did not believe me and said,

'Do *you know you could go to jail for this?, you will be taken into custody until someone takes you out on Bail. Do you want that?'* I replied that I did not commit any offence and the passport was genuine. The Officer pointed to a man and said he can give you bail and somewhere to stay.

Suddenly there came two Bengali sea men who saw us in this condition. They decided to bail us out. They then took us to their flat and found out that one of us was a relative to one of them. We started living in their flat awaiting for our report from the immigration on the validity of our passports. As they were Bengalis they looked after us,

146

providing us food and shelter and allowed us to stay for a while as this was the first time we came to West Pakistan. A so-called foreign land with a foreign language of 'Urdu', there was no Bengali speaker at all. I was the only one who could speak and understand Urdu.

The Immigration Officer had asked me earlier,

'Kuch Paysa Hai Saat Mein?' (Do you have any money with you?)

'Kaha Sein Ayia?' (Where did you get the money from?)

I said 'Jitna Paysa Hai, Ooh to Mere Liye, Sarey Paysa State Bank of Pakistan se laya gia hai' (How much money I have, is for me. It has been stamped by the State Bank of Pakistan in Dhaka)

The Officer took ALL of my money in Pound Sterling which was taken from the Bank and I had none left. We had nothing but one suitcase we were travelling to the UK with, so we slept on the floor of the small flat and took rest thanks to the Seamen.

We did not find rice and curry as this was Pakistan and only Chapatis were available. As we were not used to Chapatis we longed to eat rice. The area we were living in was not an upper class area of Karachi. There were carts on the streets selling fresh fruits and juice in trolleys and these were readily available. There were grapes, melons, blackberries, mango, lychee, coconuts juices, served in a glass with a block of ice. We really loved the taste of it and it was so refreshing in the extreme heat. We could not survive without a glass of this cold juice, but we missed our home food of rice and fish curry.

I wrote a letter to my younger brother Tutu who was in the Pakistan Military Service in Lahore. He came along with

147

some money. He knew the area well and the restaurants where we could find rice and curry! We finally went to a restaurant and ordered food but the rice was so smelly which was imported from Burma. It was not simply boiled white rice as we do it. We had no alternative but to eat it. I asked the manager and he said rice are imported from different countries. However that day we managed to eat three different dishes of food and were happy eating for a few days in local restaurants until my brother had to leave.

There were a lot of Barber shops with toilets and showers. But neither the toilets nor the barber shops were up to the usual standard we were used to back home. The toilet facilities in the flat were really bad. Every neighbourhood had a block of toilets male and female on each side of a long building. People used to stand in queues awaiting to use the toilet facilities outside. Imagine how problematic it was! We were not used to this system from where we came from as we did not live in a place so crowded as Kemari, in the city of Karachi on Hawkes Bay.

In local flats, group of people used to sleep in one room on the floor. After waking up, the bedding had to be folded up and put in the corner of the room, we had to do the same at the flat we were staying at. It was better than being held in detention without charge. Rents were not cheap for these flats and thankfully we did not have to pay thanks to our friends. People were expected to eat out, that was a norm in Kemari.

On one occasion we went to Clifton in Karachi. A beautiful beachside resort town were people would holiday from Pakistan and overseas. People would hire boats and row and have boat races. There were speed boats and people were swimming and enjoying water sports. We saw a big fayre and lots of stalls. It was a lovely sight.

In one evening, the weather was a bit cool giving us a relief from the scorching daytime weather. We were walking near to water fountain on the top floor of a shopping mall. The fountain water was coming out in different colours it was beautiful to watch. Suddenly we noticed a group of people who looked like Bengalis like us. they approached us and looked to pale and helpless. They were so happy to see us a smile broke out on their thin gloomy faces. I asked them why they looked so frail and sad.

They said that they had been there for ten weeks stranded on a transit to England. The immigration police held them, saying that their passports were forged obtained from illegal sources and kept all their money just like us! They had genuine passports too. They did not believe them either. They threatened them with a jail sentence and there was a man who bailed them out until a proper enquiry was made. The enquiry would never be made as it was utterly false.

This was sounding all too familiar to us. It seemed like this was their business to steal money. He told me, six weeks had passed for them and nothing happened. They had no money to survive, he asked for a loan to the man who gave them bail but he said

'Go and ask for money from your relatives back home or go and work in the shipping company as cleaners. You could only earn five rupees a day!'

That means he was in on it too! He was the guy who was bailing people out and his partner was the Immigration Officer! The young man told me he had no option and began cleaning like the man said. The man who bailed them out then said,

'Have you got any money from abroad to pay me for your food and accommodation? You cannot live for free as I am not a relative of yours, I don't have to buy food for you'.

He told me that the immigration officer had taken away all his belongings and money.

It suddenly dawned on me having heard his account of events that we were in a similar condition with the Immigration Officer who was earning extra income from innocent people travelling abroad. Taking money from them when they carried only a little for their journey, it was atrocious.

They had made a business of harassing people and sending a person to get them out on bail so they would unknowingly trust that person so he would extort money and use them for labour. Thank God we did not go to that person that the Immigration Office had pointed to and instead were bailed out by the Bengali sea men.

The next day, we told the Seamen about this story. We all went to confront the person who gave that young men bail and accommodation. We wanted to confront for extorting travellers. We found him prostrating at the grave of the so called Phir Sahib (Saint). I asked one of our companions to grab hold of him and take him outside the worshipping place out of respect. We threatened him saying that we would not spare his life.

'Tell us about your business with the Immigration Officer and the Police Officer'. We shouted.

He admitted all the facts. The trio were extorting money from travellers and leaving them destitute and stranding in an unknown city to befall their fate. We had fallen prey to a syndicate. I told him,

'If we are not released within the next three days, you and your partners would face the consequences. Your bodies will float in the drains in Kemari. ' I was livid.

There were ten of us in our group. After a few punches on his face and threats. He admitted that enquiries of providing our passports to be genuine were all false! A few days after, as promised, he came to the flat to see us and handed over our passports. Thank God, the beating worked wonders!

We bought tickets from KLM airlines with the help of the seamen and landed in Heathrow International Airport, London, UK at the auspicious time of 8:30pm on 19th May 1960. The whole journey from Dhaka, back to Fenchuganj because of the plane engineering issue and then transit in Pakistan was a huge trauma of over six weeks.

After leaving Karachi I starting thinking on the plane, what would happen to me in a foreign country in England. When I finally get there, will I be able to make a worthwhile career or let the days of the past chase me?

My name is Zia meaning light or lamp. I thought,

'Main hue aiysa Deepak jisme na batti na tell' the meaning of which is that I was that kind of lamp that that had no fuel left in it to generate light. What would happen now? But I had hope, surely one day it would change.

I started to think about others that would fall in the trap in Karachi, and I could not forget those we left behind. There were so many stranded there in transit. Thankfully all passport were returned to us and also the group of young men we befriended, but what about new people who were to come? When I got to England I wrote a letter of complaint to the Immigration Office and the Police in

151

Karachi about this crime but I did not get any response. I hoped that they would not continue to do this with other travellers but something tells me that this sort of thing would continue to happen.

FINAL DESTINATION

I reached England in 1960, having no plan as to what I would do here. I only knew my father's cousin lived in Coventry and I did not know how Coventry looked. I spent the first night in London, Camden town with a relative of one of the companions I had travelled from Karachi with. He helped me get a train ticket to Coventry. He took me to Euston railway station and bought me a ticket to Coventry. I had my Uncle's address written down on a scrap piece of paper and checked I had his details. I got to Coventry Station and reached his address by taxi.

When I got to his flat, he was at work, so I waited for him. He had a number of flat mates who were also from Sylhet and they fed me and chatted with me until my Uncle reached home. He was so pleased to see me when he arrived and talked a lot with me. I started to look for work and remembered my geography lessons in school about England, so I knew the names of the most famous cities and liked to go to the train and bus stations.

I became really despondent in Coventry, it was after all an industrial town and a world away from the green fields I loved. There was factory upon factory and smoke in the air. I just did not feel happy there.

The people there that I met were working in industries in various capacities. They wore boiler suits and looked dirty and untidy. They smelled of the industrial suds. I did not want to become one of them working in industries. I was looking for ways and means to find prospects in different cities. Every morning my Uncle would come and ask me, which factories have I been to and did I find a job yet? But wherever I went, I saw the notice saying 'No Vacancies'.

One day my uncle Ali said to me,

"The council is advertising for dustbin men. Can you go for this to start with?"

No appointment was required for the job. I asked him, *"What would the wages be?"*

"Seven pounds and ten shillings a week" he told me. This was for forty hours. I thought to myself one pound was equal to thirteen rupees and four anas at that time, back in Bangladesh.

"I am not willing to do this kind of job" I replied.

Did I come here to do these menial dirty jobs? I was the only person in the house who was unemployed. The others thought I was too proud to get into this work. I was not happy at all, to live in this atmosphere. I wanted to get away from Coventry. There was no direct telephone, and I could not get in touch with my father. I became quite despondent and no one else could understand my feelings. I shouted to God, the house was empty.

"Oh my God, show me mercy!" I wailed. *"I am living in uncertainty, helpless and in grief. Please help me!"*

A friend of my Uncle arrived the next day from Bedford. He has a restaurant there. He was an ex-seaman. He asked me if I was a new arrival in this country and whether I could speak English at all. I told him that I could speak a little. He advised me if I could read and write in English and speak well, then he could even offer me a job in his restaurant! Taking orders, explaining the menu and dishes to the customers etc. I told him that I would not be able to do this. I was only waiting for the day to come when I would be able to leave Coventry and try my luck elsewhere like a fortune hunter.

People living in the house started saying,

"He is a big-headed man, He won't find a job in this country!"

"His expectations are far too high!" they moaned.

This is what they thought of me. I thought I would have to prove them wrong.

UNCLE ALI

Uncle Ali used to cook for me regularly. On one weekend he found the food remained the same untouched as he had given to me.

"Do you eat everyday?" He asked me.

"I do eat everyday, but I don't like to eat meat which smells horrible" I replied.

I used to go to the grocery shop nearby and bought a bottle of milk and a tin of Mangoes. I would mix it up with cooked rice and eat it. I had no problem eating like this and I had a sweet tooth! He told me, I had to eat proper meals. This is why he cooked for me, to ensure I eat properly. I said meat or chicken are not halal here, so they are forbidden for us. The animal was slaughtered without uttering the name of God. He said, he always bought Kosher meat, the blood of the animal was drained out, therefore Muslims could eat it. It is possible to eat this kind of meat due to no proper availability of halal meat, but still I tried to avoid it. That is why I stick to milk and mangoes with rice. I was quite happy with it.

It was quite funny actually, in Sylheti language we call the shop, a shof or shaf. That word actually means snake too! Once I was so confused when my uncle asked me if I would like to eat *Shafor Ghust* meaning, meat from the shop. But it translated into meat from a snake and I got so scared! I thought he wanted me to eat a snake!

UNCLE MONN

One day there appeared a God-send. A person who was my father's first cousin. Uncle Monn, who in his student life, had lived in our village home. He had achieved a degree in commerce. He was very smartly dressed, clean shaven and study. He told me all about the Cities of Bath and Bristol and I was intrigued. He was working with The Automatic Telephone and Electric Company in Bristol. I was really impressed with his attire!

I asked him, "*Uncle would you take me with you wherever you live?*" He told me that he could not take me and that Uncle Ali would scold him.

"*You could come one day on your own to Bristol, where I live*". He told me, and left his address with me.

A couple of days later, I asked Uncle Ali, I would like to visit Uncle Monn in Bristol for a few days only. I was so happy, I took only one briefcase with me and left my suitcase in Coventry so that Uncle Ali knew I would return. I knew how to reach Bristol, I came to Birmingham New Street railway station and caught the Plymouth Express train to Bristol Temple Meads.

BRISTOL

Upon arriving in Bristol, I caught a taxi to my Uncle's place. He was very pleased to see me. I had no intention to go back to Coventry! I had the starting of a new life!

I met some young people who were very friendly. They were clean and smartly dressed working in restaurants and others in private companies. My Uncle told me to pop into the Employment Agency now known as the job centre and seek to find a job. It was Christmas time and they needed cheap labourers so I got a job almost immediately. It was a temporary job for the Christmas period at the Port of Bristol Authority. I noticed a colleague at work was working hard just like me and he told me that he was studying at Oxford University doing Engineering. I started to think why is he working a manual job when he is at Oxford University. It brought me down to earth, I realised that we have to work hard to achieve a success in life.

After the Christmas period I decided to go with a friend to Oxford and look for jobs, but I could not find anything.

I took a coach to Luton and started looking there. I found many people in Luton, doing odd jobs, mostly unemployed or manual labour work working as machine operators. I recognised that these people had left very good jobs back home in the repairing works in our local steamer repairing factory, the General Navigation and River Steamer Company in Fenchuganj, Sylhet. I wondered why people left their better jobs and top positions to come to England and do manual labour work?

A lot of my kin folk were now operating heavy machinery, drilling, welding, chapping, grinding. There were a lot of mechanical engineering factories even making car parts.

158

Britain needed cheap labourers from the commonwealth countries who had no other alternative but to work in these jobs to secure quick employment. After all they must send money back home to support their families.

When I was in Luton I was travelling to different places looking for jobs. I found a job in Welwyn Garden City at the site of installation of The Automatic Telephone Company. I worked there for a few months only travelling every day from Luton. I then found another job in Cam Gears Limited in Herefordshire, as a Cam Generator Operator manufacturing steering gears for motor vehicles. It was very hard work and I was working shifts. The wages were good, better than I had in other jobs.

One day a piece of iron stuck into my hand. It was so painful and it was bleeding heavily. I thought if I stay with this kind of job I would be a Machine Operator for the rest of my life. My cousin Nefa Bhaisab was unemployed for seven months. He was already an experienced operator who came one year before me to the UK. But the manager said, although he would like to employ him, there were no vacancies at present.

I asked him, "*If I create a vacancy would you employ him?*"

He promised he would, so I resigned from my job, creating a vacancy. He was employed in my place as Cam Generator Operator.

I did not want to be unemployed, I joined the Pakistan High Commission as a Liaison Assistant in London. But I was not paid better than the industrial employment. I left the job after a while and went to an interview in Griffiths House to work for the London Department for Transport in the Underground. The employment officer asked me

159

questions as to why I was unemployed for the last two weeks. He said to me,

'If you cannot find a job, ask your High Commission to give you a return passport and go back to where you came from'.

I got so angry and took my passport out of my pocket and showed it saying to him;

'If you can read English, see it says, the holder of this passport is proceeding to the UK for employment'. I waived it in his face angrily. I had come to see him to find a job and he was telling me this!

I said, *'I'll be better off, without your job!'.*

While coming back from that interview I reached the train station and started thinking, it was very difficult to find a job and even if I get a job it would be in manual labour. It would be better for me to start a restaurant business whereby I could be a Manager and also employ people who were in a similar position to me and that way I could somehow help others to support their families back home. We could live a better life for ourselves. I gathered some of my friends and discussed the idea. There were four of us who were interested in this idea and were trustworthy people. But we needed a lot of money to start a business. Where would I get the money from? I asked my Uncle about this. He said I was just like my father, I would be able to do a business as I was so determined. But I needed some experience.

RESTAURANT EXPERIENCE

I came back to Bristol and I had made up my mind to get some experience in a restaurant. There was a restaurant which the Partner needed to go to Bangladesh as his wife was sick. He asked me to come and run his restaurant but I had no prior experience. I would have to learn on the job. He agreed to train me up before he left, and he knew I would be perfect for the job! It was The Taj Mahal restaurant in Bristol.

There was a chef, a close friend of the other partner Mr Ahmed who was already on holiday in Bangladesh. Mr Ali introduced me to the chef as the new manager of the restaurant before he left. He told him to look after me and provide me a snack before the dinner after work. But after he had gone, the chef did not care to cook for me or make me snack. When asked, he used to say, sorry he was busy. He used to think himself an acting boss in place of his friend, Mr Ahmed. I was shocked. I promised to myself that I would make him cook for me from tomorrow! The staff were all single people living in the flat above the restaurant. One night when the restaurant was closed, they all went upstairs into their rooms. I pretended to be drunk, took an empty bottle of whisky in my hand (which I had filled with water) and shouted at the chef!

"Hey you Chef! Come out of your room!" I shouted out.

"I want to know why don't you cook for me?" I asked him. *"I will have you, I promise. I will throw you down from the top floor of the stairs down to the bottom. Did you hear me?"* I shouted. I moved left to right like I was drunk. Just pretending.

He started shivering out of fear, he was a middle-aged man quite calm and religious.

"I promise I will provide food when you want it". He told me.

"Don't forget it, or else....!" I shouted.

The head waiter's room was next door to the chef's room. He was standing near to the chef and whispered into his ear, *"That Mr Chowdhury was always so gentle and well behaved. How come he was drinking alcohol and got absolutely drunk when he knew that drinking alcohol was strictly forbidden for Muslims. He comes from a good family, I just cannot believe he would do such a thing"*.

Someone else said to him, *"You don't know Mr Chowdhury. When he's angry, he can do anything. He does not care about anyone or anything at that time!"* the staff knew the truth about me.

From the next day onward, he never failed to make food for me and always asked what I would like to eat.

HAMID

One evening I came to meet a young man. He was about 30 years old and his name was Hamid. He was an Orphan from Calcutta, and originally a Punjabi.

During his childhood he had lost both of his parents, he had no place to live or any shelter. He had been living anywhere, on the streets and wherever he could find a place. He became rough and had to survive the streets by fighting other such kids. He was hated, cursed, beaten and even stabbed by a knife on many occasions. He had to fight to survive in this turmoil.

He to me that he went to the seaman's recruiting office in Calcutta seeking a job of any kind on overseas vessels. He got a job as an orderly of the Captain of the ship. He arrived in Liverpool, the Captain absolutely loved him as he was most obedient and trust worthy. He came to England and ended up in Bristol.

I found him looking helplessly in front of the Taj Mahal Restaurant in Stokescroft. I was out for some fresh air and found his looking at the door of the restaurant.

I invited him in, he was so pleased to see me so welcoming. He got into the restaurant. I offered him a cup of tea and food and had asked him to stay overnight. He smiled and accepted my offer and slept soundly that night.

He came to me the next morning and thanked me for the food and shelter. He found us preparing for the opening of the restaurant and asked me if he could help us with anything. He then started hoovering the floor and changing the tablecloths with us. He also went to the kitchen and helped the kitchen staff by washing dishes

163

and cleaning. We actually did need an extra pair of hands and though he would be a great addition. He asked me if he could give us a hand everyday. I quite happily agreed. At the end of the week I offered him some money with the rest of the staff, but he did not want to accept.

He said "*I don't want any money, I have no one to look after. I am alone in this world, I simply want to live happily*".

I said "*Yes you need some money to buy things for yourself. Things you will need like clothes, toothbrush and paste and essential things*".

He accepted the job as a kitchen porter at the Taj Mahal restaurant. A few weeks later, the cook decided to leave and Hamid took his place. The head waiter said to me,

"*How come you entrusted Hamid with cooking for the customers? It needs a long experienced hand to do the job*". Hamid over heard this and became angry. He said "*If I can't do the cooking properly like a proper cook then you can through me out!*" He exclaimed. By this time the other Partner Mr Ahmed returned back to the restaurant, he did not say anything.

After two months the chef had left and Hamid took over for him too. He carried on as Chef and there were no complaints from the customers at all! He was a excellent chef, very quick and intelligent. In such a short time he had progressed through the ranks. We were very impressed. At the end he found some friends and was looking for a shop premises to open his own restaurant. Mr Ahmed, the partner used to come to the restaurant sometimes with his wife for a visit. He heard from someone that Hamid was going to open a restaurant. Traditionally any worker leaving to open another such business in competition could get the sack! Mr Ahmed did exactly that, although Hamid did not sign any lease for a restaurant. Yet he was sacked from his position for planning to open a restaurant himself.

Hamid was really angry and upset by this. He threatened the boss saying he would take revenge. I said to the boss that Hamid should stay until he opens his restaurant, as I was representing the other Partner. But Hamid did not want to stay any longer and left saying he would teach Mr Ahmed a lesson.

I helped Hamid to find somewhere else to live and a new job at my friend's place. One day he went to Sir Alfred McAlpine building projects and found a job at a building site. After three months he was given the position of a Ganger to manage some labourers. He then went to Bangladesh to get married but found it very difficult to find a bride without any formal background.

One father said he would need to deposit ten thousand pounds in his bank account to marry his daughter. He was distraught and shouted, "Do you want to sell your daughter!". Hearing the commotion the police sub-inspector has been nearby and asked what happened.

Hamid explained his life story and the inspector believed his sincerity and ignored his arrogance. He offered to give his own daughter's hand in marriage to Hamid!

Hamid called me from Bangladesh and told me the news, I told him to go ahead and get married! He helped him with his immigration application for his wife and she entered England. They were a lovely couple and she became a translator here in the UK. He used to say, he had only one friend in the world like a brother. When he passed away many years later, I lost a true friend.

THE PAKISTAN WELFARE ASSOCIATION

I joined the Pakistan Welfare Association in Bristol. All the restaurant owners were Bangladeshis but we did not have independence yet. The Pakistanis at the Association did not like that East Pakistanis had joined. So later on in 1970 we started our own community organisation named Bangladesh Welfare Association. It was 1962 that I received a telegram from my father, saying I need to send the plane fare for my younger brother Jitu to come to the UK before the Act of Parliament is passed. The Immigration Act 1962 which would mean a visa will be required for travel and work. My brother should come now while you only need a passport to come to the UK. I was only a waiter and had to borrow money from friends to send the plane fare. He came to the UK and joined as a waiter in Taj Mahal in Bristol with me.

Leaving Jitu in my place, I started going from town to town looking for premises to open a restaurant. He was very sharp and learned the job very quickly. I visited Taunton, Exeter, Southampton, Torquay, Taigmouth, Plymouth and the City of Bath. The last place attracted me so much, it was unique and picturesque. Finally, I set my mind to opening a restaurant in Bath where the romans built the city almost as a replica of Rome itself. The buildings where made of bathonian stone, white and grand. Lord Clive, the Governor General of India came and settled here after his return to England.

The river Avon passes underneath the Putney Bridge. Standing on the bridge I would look to the stream of water, trickling down the hills it was so beautiful and eye-catching. I was attracted to the city and its unique beauty and historical nature. Opposite was the pavilion which stands by a small botanical park full of a floral array of exotic flowers. There were pansies, lilies, dahlia of pinks,

166

red, yellow and white. I said to myself, I did not come to England for business, but if I ever open a business when it will be a restaurant nestled in the beautiful city of Bath on Avon.

BUSINESS PARTNERS

It was 1963, I got together with a few people who had restaurant experience. There were four of us and we decided to set up a partnership. One was capable of being a chef, one a restaurant manager, one waiter and another who was a trainee engineering student. I did some research and spoke to some people already working in restaurants and others who owned restaurants. With little money and no experience in the restaurant business we started off. I was the one who did not have enough money to put in to the partnership but I had the determination and skill to open the restaurant without any practical skills in customer service or restaurant management. The others were happy to input some money.

My three partners had some money saved, and we went to the Bank and obtained a bank loan for the rest. I opened a business account as asked by the Manager of the Bank. I found a derelict Wine Merchants which we purchased freehold. It was a three-storey building and needed a lot of work. We obtained quotations from the builder and started the work, we when refurbished it with carpets and furniture. It was converted into a high-class Moghul style dining suite.

We named the restaurant, the Taj Mahal of Bath. The meaning behind the name was a tribute to the real Taj Mahal sat in India, built by the Emperor Shajahan on the grave of his wife Mumtaj. It is a great wonder of the world.

The Taj Mahal of Bath was photographed in the newspapers and the grand opening as attended to by Mr Savage, the chief guest from the BBC. He named it '*The best restaurant in the west*'.

168

We donated our first takings to charity and did this as a regular habit. I did not give up my studies throughout this time. I was a student, I studying Office Organisation and Management and another course Sales and Marketing in The City of Bath Technical College and Transport in Bristol College of Commerce. Business was boomed, our reputation spread all over the country and everyone wanted to come and visit the Taj Mahal of Bath.

It was a most joyous time in my life but not without struggle and hard work.

HOOLIGANS

Whilst managing the restaurant in Bath, we came across a few issues.

On one Saturday night, the restaurant was at full capacity. There was no room for any more customers. I was guarding the door, at about eleven thirty p.m. a group of drunken people pushed the door forcibly and entered into my restaurant. I was unable to do anything. They were all big, broad, rugby players who were coming straight from a national rugby competition in Gloucester.

I told them we had no more tables available but they would not listen. They told me not to talk nonsense. They were so rude and unruly and did not listen to any of us. They picked up our water jugs and tumblers full of water from the table and threw them in the air towards the ceiling! Some of them went to the WC and smashed the toilet fans, tried to pull the hand basins out and smash the toilets.

When the head waiter, my brother Jitu, asked them to leave the premises, they grabbed him by the neck and punched him in the nose! He started bleeding immediately. They bounded into the kitchen and when the Chef asked them to leave, they punched him in the face too! There was a chaos and racket caused by these people. Some customers walked out of the restaurant without paying the bill and some did not bother to enter the restaurant seeing the commotion inside.

Somebody called the police and four policemen arrived within a few minutes. They found someone had been stabbed in the back! It was one of the rugby players. The police took all of my staff to the police station and put them in a cell all night, suspecting them of stabbing the player.

I bailed them out the next morning. I tried to consult a solicitor to defend the staff but none would accept our case. They thought that one of my staff must have stabbed the player.

The solicitor advised the staff to admit the crime, but I said,

"We did not cause the injury at all, why would we admit liability for this?".

At long last one solicitor who just finished his training, agreed to take our case. I told him, there was a fight in front of the York Hotel about thirty yards away from my restaurant. At approximately, eleven p.m. there was a fight and there were three police vehicles who attended. The police must have a record of the incident. The group surely came from there and I asked the solicitor to obtain the police record to come this.

I told him, the policemen who attended my restaurant during the chaos arrested all my staff and took all the silverware from the tables and the knives from the kitchen to produce as evidence of the stabbing.

At court, a doctor who examined the injury before the magistrates said the depth of the injury could not have been caused by the restaurant knives, the kitchen knives or the table knives at the Taj Mahal. The police confirmed that there had been a huge fight in front of the York Hotel. The injury must have happened there or elsewhere, not at my restaurant. The size of the injury did not match with the depth and size of the knives at our restaurant.

Alas, the charge of stabbing, brought against the restaurant staff was dismissed and all were acquitted and released. The case was featured in the Evening Mail, the Daily Mail, the Evening Chronical of Bath and all newspapers mentioning the restaurant, myself and my staff and the name of the solicitor's firm which became famous and enhanced its reputation along with our restaurant.

Watching this court case, I thought to myself, one day I would like to sit on the magistrate's bench as a Justice of Peace and adjudicate matters such as these. As a student I used to go to court to watch my uncle who was a magistrate. I also used to attend various courts with my father who was a land owner and dealt with many of his own cases in person on land matters. My wish came true in 1992 when I became the first Bangladeshi to be appointed as a Justice of the Peace in Birmingham.

THE INCREDIBLE FORCE OF ALICE

In 1964, I purchased a second freehold property and opened another restaurant, 'Taj Mahal of Weston Supermare' which was in a perfect beachfront location on the Weston Supermare peninsula. It was originally a Greek Restaurant and I converted it into an Indian Restaurant. I did not have any Partners in this business, only myself as the sole proprietor. The restaurant was in a picturesque spot, the only Indian restaurant in the whole of the seaside town and we were insanely busy with full seats on most nights. My brother Jitu was in the management of this restaurant and his wife Alice was the head waitress along with two other waitresses. There were many different kinds of customers, on one Friday my brother and the staff were serving food in the restaurant. Three young men came to have dinner. After finishing their meals, they were looking around suspiciously, looking here and there. In a swift moment when the waitress was busy behind the counter, they found an opportunity to quickly leave their table and run out of the restaurant without paying their bills!

Alice and my brother ran after them, she caught one of them and grabbed him phone a telephone booth by the roadside. The other two were hiding behind the sandy mounds on the beach. The one caught by Alice tried his utmost to get loose and escape, by Alice was a very strong lady! She dragged him by the ear back down the street and to the restaurant, sat him back down at the table and made him pay the bill! He admitted that he had done this in many restaurants and got away with it, but not this time. This was the first time he actually paid for his meal in a restaurant! A lot of this kind of thing went on after the new Severn Bridge was constructed which connected England and Wales and brought in different kinds of people to the seaside town of Weston Supermare.

HOMECOMING

In 1965 I started to get tired and homesick, I really needed a break after opening two restaurants. I missed my parents, I longed to see them and my siblings. I decided to go home for a vacation. I talked to my partner and he agreed it was time I could take a break, he could read my mind. I booked a ticket for Dhaka in advance.

At that time, a war between India and Pakistan had broken out. As a result, Pakistan International Airlines flights were cancelled. They were not allowed to fly over India and violate its airspace. India refused to vacate their airspace for the aircrafts to pass through to East Pakistan and I had to re-arrange the flight for a few months later when things settled a little, but some restrictions still remained.

When I finally reached Dhaka it had taken me seven hours journey as the aircraft had to fly over a Sri-Lanka and the Bay of Bengal.

I met my father in Dhaka and we travelled back to Fenchuganj together by train. It was the first time I was seeing him in five years. Whilst sitting in the train I started to think how East Pakistan would be saved if India ever attacked. It would take Pakistani Soldiers seven hours to come and rescue East Pakistan as West Pakistani Soldiers would not be allowed to fly over India airspace which it situated in the middle between the two sides of Pakistan!

WINE IN THE MUD

Back at home in Bangladesh, one evening I found more and more people from the village heading towards our Tongi (out-house). I was wondering why all these people were gathering together. There must have been a dispute, a fight or something else of a serious nature to be adjudicated by my father. I asked one person why all the people has congregated here.

I was told that a young man of this village (our tenant), was ploughing the field and was seen drinking alcohol whilst resting at the edge of the ploughing field. They brought the accused person before my father for punishment. That was an interesting incident for me, especially having returned home after five years living in the UK.

My father heard the charges against the accused, and heard his admission of guilt that he had drank a bottle of beer whilst on his break. And secondly he had buried this bottle underground into the mud to get ice cold on a hot summer's day. He admitted he had done this previously on two occasions. The sentencing order was given by my father at the end of the hearing. The accused would hold his ears by his hands and go around the assembled people present announcing the offence committed and that he would not repeat such an offence ever again. He apologised to the community in this fashion.

In those days the land owners had to deliver a punishment showing the accused as disgraced before the community as a deterrent to others not to make the same mistake. Petty disputes and committal of crimes of this nature were dealt with in this way by the land owners or by the chairman of the union council elected outside the courts. The system still continues to be carried out today.

175

THE OTTER'S STORY

There was a big pond in front of our house called the Fukri (in Sylheti). There were all kinds of tropical fish, even fish from Cambodia, Thailand and other countries. These attracted the otters from the nearby hills, they came at night when it was quiet. They wanted to catch the fish and eat them!

Every morning we used to see fish bones and half eaten fish lying down on the sides of the pond. As such the fish started to vanish day by day. We hardly heard the sound of the fish splashing around from our Tongi anymore. My father investigated the disappearance of the fish and employed experts to look into the matter. They confirmed it was indeed the Otters who were responsible.

The experts put a special kind of power into the pond to deter the otters from coming to the pond and keep the fish in tact.

At this some otters did not come near the pond and others that did come were found lying on the banks of the pond as the fish had been. That was how we got rid of the enemy of the fish and saved them all!

We could once again hear the happy fish splashing around the pond. But how long would this last? We really needed our very own Pied Piper of Hamelin!

MARRIAGE PROPOSALS

At home in Fenchuganj, I usually slept in my father's room. One night my father said to me,

"Oh Yes...I have to go to see a friend of mine in the Bar Library at the Courts in Sylhet. He is an Advocate who practises in Sylhet Judges Court. He asked to see you when you return home from the UK".

I wondered what he wanted to see me about. So, I went with my father the next day and met with his friend. We sat together and started talking over a cup of tea in the Bar library. He asked me several questions about what I was doing in England. He also asked which courses I had studied and what sort of business I was involved in together with my future plans.

While returning from there I said to my father *"I think I have seen him in 1949-50 visiting our house"*. He had been an inspector of Customs and Excise at that time. He had been on an inspection to Sham's house, (one of our tenants) regarding an accusation that Sham was making homemade wine without a permit. My father asked how did I manage to remember this from fifteen years ago!

At night my father showed me a yearbook of a college in Sylhet and showed me a picture of a girl in the magazine. She was the Assistant Editor of the Ushoshi magazine of MC College in Sylhet.

"How does she look?" He asked me.

"Not bad" I replied. I did not know why he was asking me this. But I further commented,

"She is a bit skinny and thin isn't she?".

This picture reminded me of a girl I had seen before. Standing with other visitors in the hospital who came to see me whilst I was ill during my childhood. I remember lying in bed and looking over at the visitors and noticing her. She was a little girl wearing a frock. Surely this was not a coincidence!

My father laughed and said, *"How can it be? She was not born at that time!"*. She informed me that she is studying science at MC College.

"She is the daughter of my friend, the Advocate you met yesterday at the Bar library". He told me.

He informed me that he had chosen her for me to get married to. I told him I was not ready to get married and did not have any extra money with me to plan a wedding celebration! My father said not to worry about that. It was his friend and they would sort something out.

I had no plan to get married but I expressed my willingness affirmatively. I don't know why I had a feeling that she would be suitable for me to be my life partner.

My brother in law (my sister's husband) insisted I should go and meet her at the college gate.

I told him that it would not be necessary. My father knew her family well, their culture, tradition and status and I believed he had chosen the right match for me. No one knew me better than my father. The matrimonial relationship is not just between a man and a woman. It involves an integration between two families in our culture.

I had a feeling that she would be a blessing in my life. I would be happy. Our families matched and my father believed our personalities would be a good match for each other. Our marriage was fixed for the 20th day of December 1965.

TRADITIONAL HAIR CUT BEFORE MARRIAGE

The day of my marriage was nearing at hand. I had my hair cut as per the family tradition by our family barber. I already had it cut at the salon in Sylhet and I forgot I was supposed to follow the tradition! When I came home after my hair cut, my father asked me why I had done it elsewhere. I was to have my hair cut by our own family barber at home. It was a traditional task for the barber from time immemorial and they waited for how would be chosen amongst them to be the lucky barber to do auspicious task.

My father told me that I had breached our age long family tradition. He said I have just done what I liked and didn't even ask! I apologised to my father and told him that I had forgotten but I would let them cut it again no problem. He said, I better do that!

A week before the wedding, Ishwar the barber came to cut my hair. I told him that I had been waiting for him to come but he said my hair was already cut! I laughed and said no it needed the final touch by him and he was so happy.

*

WHERE TO PUT THE BRIDE?

I was really worried about the upcoming wedding and how I would manage the costs. I didn't bring much money back with me from the UK and there was not much space at our home in Fenchuganj.

We had a sister in law already at home, my younger brother Tutu who was in the military had married a year and a half before me.

I asked my cousin Nefa Bhaisab to speak to my father about this. I prepared him before hand and told him to raise the subject of where the new bride will stay. I did not want to ask him directly.

We went to see my father and Nefa Bhaisab started talking about the wedding in general. He then broached the subject of accommodation and where everyone would be staying. He then asked where the bride will be brought home to and where she would live. My father laughed and told us not to worry, he would simply make another house!

I wondered how this would be possible but true to his word a house was build with wood with a metal roof within twelve days!

I simply could not believe it.

*

NIGHT BEFORE THE WEDDING

It was in the afternoon, the day before my wedding when I was called to the open forecourt of our main building.

Hundreds of people were assembled within the grounds. Many people including our tenants who would not be going to the wedding. As per marriage traditions in Bangladesh, I was placed on a decorated chair.

I had my hands and feet washed and one of my aunts wiped my face and hands with a special grass called a 'Dubra' collected from a place out of the reach of cows, goats, sheep and horses who might eat it. Then another aunt made a small paste of turmeric and water which she used as a kind of mask for my face and hands with the Dubra grass as a brush. This was meant to make my face glow for the wedding.

I was given a special cold sweet and sour drink. Then I had a break to take a shower and wash the turmeric off my body. After doing so I had to dress up in my wedding clothes to show the audience how I would look tomorrow at the wedding. This was done to allow everyone to join in with the wedding festivities even those who would not see me at the wedding tomorrow.

Once dressed in my smart wedding clothes I was led to a curved grand chair and sat down on it like a king with an audience. I wore a dazzling diamante sherwani (Indian suit) which I had hired, along with a turban and pointy matching Nagrai shoes, I looked like a famous Nawaab!

Everyone was smiling and congratulated me. My aunt came with the Mendhi which was crushed leaves to make a paste that serves as a dye, when applied to skin it looks like a decorative tattoo but is traditionally used in weddings. It was applied to my right hand, a circle was

181

drawn with the mehndi in my palm and on my little finger. I would have to wait for it to dry for a few hours, whilst sitting on my chair and enjoying the party. Every now and then guests would come and place a mithai (sweet meat) into my mouth and wish me luck for tomorrow with their blessings. I was feeling really excited and nervous too. But I was happy.

After a while it was time for me to bid farewell to everyone and I said my goodbyes and left to wash off my mehndi. I saw a red stain like a round circle in my palm and my finger. It symbolises that I am the Groom.

MARRIAGE

I got married on 20th December 1965 with the blessings of Almighty God and I am still happy.

In the morning we got up quite early to make the journey to Sylhet from Fenchuganj, some thirty to forty people accompanied us and the rest remained at home waiting for the wedding party to return. Other guests would join us in Sylhet at the wedding, which was in a marquee erected at the Bride's house accommodating around 150 people.

Traditionally the groom should have pilau rice with a figure of a chicken or a hen on a huge platter and share it with his friends and family members. It was a tradition called the 'Shagorana'. At our house we simply did not have time for this and prepare for our journey so we had some pilau rice and snacks and set of for the train. We were supposed to take our groom's men with us to Sylhet at our cost, but I only had the money for the journey there!

I was so anxious about this, during the whole day I was wondering how we would bring these people back home. In the end the money I received from my in laws for our wedding present (Salami) was enough to pay for everyone's train ride home and some of the wedding costs. I was saved!

Once I reached Sylhet I got to my uncle's house where I had lived before. The family had already come to Fenchuganj leaving only my uncle there in the house alone. He did not have any help at home and had never made a cup of tea in his life. I was so hungry that Nefa Bhaisab suggested we go to his sister's house. She gave us whatever she had and we ate very happily there before setting off to the bride's house.

We took a general taxi to the house, not a decorated groom's hire car or anything like that. We arrived and I sat with all the guests in the marquee outside. A Moulana (priest) came and sat with his marriage registry book in front of him. He asked me in front of witnesses three times if I was in agreement to marry the bride. He had already done this with the bride before coming to me. We both agreed and the marriage was solemnised with the blessings of our family.

At the end of the party I was taken inside the house with a few people to meet the bride. At that time we did not look at each other it was frowned upon, so we sat next to each other and someone brought a mirror and placed it on the floor where my wife was looking down. I was told I could look at the mirror to see my wife's face but I didn't. I was happy with my father's decision and I didn't need to look. We were made to exchange cups of milk and sweet meats with each other without looking at one another. Today it seems absurd but it was normal in those days.

We took a car to the train station and there was a compartment for the bride and groom. My wife did not say anything at all on the train journey. It was a forty five minute journey to Fenchuganj and we were greeted by two Palki's (Palanquins). These were traditionally hand-crafted wooden carriages made specifically for a bride or groom. There were always beautifully painted decorations on all sides using red, pink, yellow and other colours celebrating the happy occasion of marriage.

The bride sat in one and I sat in another and it was lifted into the air and carried by four men to our home. I made a lot of problem here, I did not want to get inside the Palki at all. It was a small box on two stilts and I thought I would fall out of it. I got out a few times and walked most of the way home whilst they carried my wife adjacent to me in her Palki. Before we reached home I got inside my Palki before I got shouted at by everyone as we were not allowed to walk on the ground as bride and groom, according to tradition. We still have those two Palanquins in Fenchuganj today which are now obsolete. But we keep them as souvenirs and artifacts of our history.

When we reached home, I thought the wedding was over so I went into my room and got changed into my lungi and t-shirt which were my night clothes. Suddenly I heard someone calling for me, everyone had been looking for me! I did not enter the house with the bride as I should have done and my sisters and sister-in-law had taken her inside. I joined in my night clothes and we sat on two stools. At that time we did not have any decorations and it was very plain. We again exchanged some sherbet and sweets for all to see and were asked to pray Namaaz together.

When we sat down finally, it was time for our first conversation. I told her I was the eldest son and I had a lot of responsibility in my family. I also told her I didn't have much money and in fact I had five thousand pounds of debts. She simply nodded. I did not have the money to buy her wedding

jewellery on that day but she came with gold that her father had given and some wedding gifts. She sold that gold later on for us both to go to Hajj on our holy pilgrimage. My wife has never asked me for anything to this day and has always supported me.

FIRA JATRA

As per our tradition, the Bride had come home to my house with some of her close friends or bridesmaids. They stayed with her in the room and they would chat and eat together. This was so that the bride would not feel uncomfortable in a new place and have some comfort from her friends to help her settle down.

After three days, the bride's family would come to eat a grand meal at our home and then take us both with them to stay a few days at the bride's parents house. This is called Fira-Jatra (returning home). After spending two days at my wife's parents house, my own family and relatives, about fifty women and children came to my in laws to have a grand meal, stay the night and take us back to Fenchuganj the next morning.

Traditionally all the guests remained in our house through all of these festivities and our house was full of people and laughter for many days of the wedding. It was really a grand occasion.

The holy month of Ramadhan came straight after my wedding and my father in law sent an abundance of food, snacks, fruit and sweets to us for iftar when we break our fasts. It was enough to feed our whole village!

After the month ended it was time for Eid celebration and that was a time of great joy in my life.

MY WIFE IN ENGLAND

Three months after the marriage my wife came to England, it was May 1966. I was living in the City of Bath, England, UK. I was a student as well as running two restaurant businesses in Bath and Weston Supermare. At that time, she was the only Bengali woman in Bath, and the whole of West England from East Pakistan, now Bangladesh.

She came with a great hope but she had nothing of the sort. She became bored and sad. I was busy with my businesses and studies. She was absolutely lonely. I had her admitted into Bath Technical College to do A Levels in Science subjects. In Bangladesh she had been studying the HSC and left just before the final exam. Even she could not find a female student apart from one from Kenya who became her only friend. She became so sad as if life became a burden for her. I could not bear to see this. Studying helped for a while but she was not happy.

In June 1967 our son Saadi was born. We then moved to Weston Supermare with the baby to run the business. We truly enjoyed the time at the seaside. My baby son fell ill and I took him to see the Doctor. He said we worry too much as he was my first baby and he laughed me away. The next day his condition was so serious that we spent the night taking him on our laps in turns. He had very strong diahorrea and became dehydrated, weak and limp and was not breathing properly. We got so worried and took him back to the Doctors office.

This time he telephoned the Children's hospital which was about five or six miles away from Weston Supermare. It was an isolated children's hospital, the ambulance came and took him there. He was checked in and was given a bed as arranged by the Doctor. At that time they did not allow us to stay by his bedside, so we had to leave him there.

The next day, we went to the hospital and found him screaming. His small head had gotten stuck between the bars of the cot. We reported this to the nurse who dislodged him! He stayed there for about ten days and was released. He had infectious diahorrea. We used to take him out for fresh air by the sea in a pram. When the winter came and business became quiet. We had to close the business and went back to Bath with the family.

We used to live in the flat upstairs of the restaurant, I used to come and find her weeping all alone. There was no one to be with her for a little bit

of mental support. In 1968 I took her back to her parents in Bangladesh with Saadi. She lived with her parents and two younger sisters who would help her look after the baby. She joined college again in Sylhet.

CHANGE OF PLANS

I came back to UK and became a full-time student at Birmingham University studying Law.

I had the burden of running two restaurants businesses, I had to go to Bath on the evening of Friday to work the weekend after classes. I worked at a very busy restaurant on Friday nights and went to Weston Supermare to work in the second restaurant on Saturday nights. I was living in the Halls of Residence at Birmingham University with regular absence from the halls on weekends.

The Tutor reported this to the Head of the Law Faculty and I was warned to stick to studies, unfortunately I had to say that 'Business is my bread and butter' and I could not stick to only studies.

He said *'You only have one option. To withdraw from the faculty'*. Reluctantly I had to withdraw from my courses.

I decided to study Judicial Administration in a short course, at the same university instead.

My wife passed her exams with flying colours and was awarded a scholarship to start her BA Honours Degree in English.

In 1970 I went back to Sylhet to settle down permanently thinking that my wife, after her Master's Degree would become a lecturer in the girls' college and I could complete my LLB Law degree in Bangladesh to practice law as an Advocate. I left the business in UK to my brother to run and I thought we could have a happy life together in Bangladesh. I planned that my son would be going to a private school in Sylhet. I thought I had left the business in good hands and we would travel to the UK on holidays. But fate had a different hand to play.

MY SON

When I arrived in Bangladesh I found my two and half year old son had come to the airport in Dhaka to receive me with his mother, my sister and also her husband.

In the morning, when he saw me sleeping in the same bed he got scared and frightened. At breakfast time, he was missing and no one could find him. We searched for him in every corner of the house but could not find him at all.

We were so worried about what had happened to him. All of a sudden a domestic worker, Fitkiri found him hiding under a bed in a small room. He was taken out, but he was scared and shivering clutching a blanket.

How quickly a small child can forget!

We used to spend time together in our flat above the restaurant. When he was sick, I used to hold him in my arms all night and fall asleep sometimes, waking with a jolt to make sure I didn't drop him.

At that time, I recalled a historical story of the Emperor of Delhi, Barber whose child Humayun was very sick. He had held him in his lap and prayed to God to take his life and let his son live. In the story God did take the father and Humayun came to the throne and became King. When Saadi was really ill and suffering, I had prayed to God to take my life and let my son live just like in the story. But God saved us both.

It took him several months to be acquainted with me and accept me as his father again.

ANGLING

A few days after, we came back to our village home in Fenchuganj, Bari. We had a lot of fun. My Dulabhai came to our bari for a holiday. We had working in the American consulate in Dhaka. My father used to breed different kinds of fish in our pond. My brother in law was fond of angling. Together we went for angling in the pond, we had to be extremely careful not to retain the small fish we caught. We had to throw them back in to grow bigger. We caught one fish every five to seven minutes. It was so exciting.

There were too many fish so we had to stock some in our bathroom water tank. This is the water supply for the house. The floor was fitted with Moroccan tiles. The splashing sound of the fish and their falling off to the floor was so noisy we could hardly sleep in the bedroom nearby. The fish came out onto the bathroom through the opening of the door and went to the back garden and started flapping on the grass. We had to catch them. My father had already warned us not to catch too many fish from the pond to avoid this kind on incident!

But it was so enjoyable we just could not help it!

THE WILD CAT

One day my Dulabhai Mr Habib and myself went cycling through the village road. After about four or five miles distance from our home we had to stop, a peculiar noise was coming out from a half constructed building on our land on a small hill. It had been left unused for many years as the Government would acquire unused land under the Land Acquisition Act at the time. Before the enforcement of the Act, my father had converted one side of the hill as a horticultural garden. He had intended to build a guest house on the other side which was only half done at the time.

At this time he was taken ill and was hospitalised after a heart attack to Sylhet under the care of a heart specialist. The building meant to become a guest house was left incomplete. It remained empty and unused. It became virtually a shelter home for wild cats to duel! The wild cats looked like little tigers but smaller in size. They had tiger like stripe on their skin and their faces looked like a tiger's. They occupied the loft section and started living there comfortably without any disturbance. They were ever so noisy, there was no human habitation in the immediate vicinity.

We quietly approached to the isolated building. I climbed the downpipe of the building and looked to the ceiling. It was too dark, nothing was visible at all. I could see the dazzling eyes of some sort of animal. I looked at the concentrated eyes in multiple and they started coming towards me. They jumped down from the loft onto the ground in front of us. I got scared and shot with the double barrel gun I had with me. The people from distance houses started coming in to find what was going on. At the gun shot, many of the wild cats scattered and bolted here and there. One of us had a torch light, I used it and climbed up and found the upper floor loft area of the building was full of chicken bones and feathers spread everywhere! The cats had stolen the local neighbourhood chickens! How cheeky!

After my father recovered, he completed the building into a guest house as planned. Gradually the area became well developed with proper roads and social and educational facilities. The horticultural garden is now called Delwar Hussain Chowdhury Horticultural garden after my father.

FIRE ON THE CHITTAGANJ EXPRESS

In 1970 I had to go to Chittaganj to see my uncle and to have the delivery of some of the household items I sent by ship from England. I had planned to shift back to Bangladesh and settle. I was on the Chittaganj express train form Sylhet. After the train departed I could sense a burning smell.

I complained to the guard of the train who went to see the station master at Kulaura railway junction. The train had stopped for nearly half and hour there. The station master brought a man, he was an electrical engineer who he said would be going with me by train upto Akhaura station, a six hour journey approximately.

There was a huge commotion and people wanted to beat up the railway guard. I wanted to help him. I started shouted with a loud voice, there were a lot of people who were on the train with me. Some of them supported me. I had hundreds of people around me.

The railway police heard my shouts and the guard of the train came. I had explained the whole story to them, they were about to kill the railway guard because he had not controlled the fire at the correct time. I told them it was not the responsibility of the guard alone for the fire containment. We can only spare his life, if he gave us the assurance that the chain of the train was working.

On the way the train was bending around the railway, we found there was a massive fire caught in our next compartment. I pulled the chain to stop the running train. The train as usual stopped at Akhaura station, with the fire blazing and we all escaped.

People stopped making so much noise as a brutal army general Tikka Khan had taken over the Governorship of the province of Bangladesh and people were in fear as he would shoot first and ask questions later. To him human lives were like cattle, and the arms in his hands were mere toys.

They were frightened to death before their actual death!

RETURN FROM CHITTAGANJ

After a week in Chittaganj, I was coming back home to Sylhet. There was another fire on the train but this time it was more forceful. The train had stopped by the outer signal while approaching Lacksham railway junction and was whistling. The train stopped in the paddy field by a natural lake. Many people and porters, rickshaw drivers, taxi drivers, and others ran with tins and cans full of water on the spot to put the fire out with water from the nearby lake. The fire was eventually out completely.

I was not alone on my journey, my uncle sent one of my cousins with me the whole way to Sylhet. He was a trainee police officer. I told him I would like to make some fun on the train. He asked me how, and I told him to wait and see. It was the time of a huge political upheaval against the government for the independence of Bangladesh. The demonstrations against the government were going on everywhere.

I stood up from my seat on the train and asked the people,

'Which political party do you belong to?'

They replied, 'Awamileague!'.

I said to them opening the train window, 'Do you want to demonstrate this with slogans?'

They replied 'Yes!'.

Awamileague is the party for the general people. As the train was stopped, there were a lot of people surrounding the train. I screamed out, 'why are you circling the train, do you want to demonstrate? Can you surround the train and tell us who put the fire out?'

196

We all started a chant stamping our feet and hands,

'WE WANT BANGLADESH! WHO PUT THE FIRE OUT?
AWAMILEAGUE! AWAMILEAGE!'

We demonstrated this for some time after the fire was put out both the people in the train and those outside. the engine started whistling to leave, the station signal turned green but the train was not moving because of the crowd around the train and they were all looking to me.

I said to them, *"Brothers, you have done a great job! Thanks for bravery, courage, it is time for us to go!"*

After that the train left to reach the next station and we chanted from station to station until we reached Sylhet. Although I did not belong to a political party, I did it for fun. My cousin asked me, where did you get the idea do to this from. I told him I learned it from Bangladesh! He asked me if we do this in England and I told him it was not necessary there.

The train left the station towards Sylhet passing one after another station until it reached Srimagal.

SRIMANGAL

Having reached Srimagal station we met another adversity. One oncoming train coming from Sylhet had become derailed!

Luckily the passengers had not been seriously hurt by the derailment. Some of them were injured and some of us were very hungry. Our snacks in the tiffin box were all finished. Children had no food or drink and it was a sorry sight, they were crying for something to eat or drink.

The canteens by the side of the road had run out of food and we could not get hold of any snacks at all. Even the drinks were finished. The small takeaway shops had nothing to offer us. After about four hours the railway line was fixed by the engineers and cleared for the train to take its journey again. We finally arrived in Sylhet after such a hectic journey.

THE BOLD SON

After returning home from Chittaganj I heard that one of my cousins who was been a village Head after the death of his father was killed by a Major of the Pakistan Army, Tikka Khan. This time his son was called in and he went with two people with him. But never returned home. He was a newly married young man who did not take any part with any political party. He was known to his villagers and people outside the village. The army must have thought that he had been supporting the liberation army by sending his people to India to get trained to fight out the Pakistani soldiers and free East Pakistan from the so called federal republic of Pakistan.

On another occasion I was going from Sylhet to Fenchuganj. At Sylhet railway station I found there was a train about to leave the station for Chatthak, the cement manufacturing plant. There was no room even on the roof of the train, it was completely jammed and crowded. The police was beating the passengers to come down from the roof of the train as it was dangerous to travel this way. There was no other train available except this one on that day. I asked the police, who gave this order of beating the public,

I said *'Stop it! Go and tell him, if the police behave like this, there would be a massacre. The public in general would beat back the police in retaliation in you treat them this way'.*

The police went back and told the Officer that someone told them to stop this or else the lives of many people would be at stake.

I said 'That man has no capacity to provide another train for the people but had the power to beat the people? He deserves to face the consequences'.

I was only a member of the public, my harsh behaviour with a loud voice and warning to the police indicated that I was someone of importance in a government department. The Officer kept quiet. The police seized their abrupt attitude. After this our train started to leave the station.

When I reached home, my father said to me;

"*Good Job you came, I invited the sub-divisional Officer who was the chief administrative head of the sub-division from Sylhet and is in fact in charge of Fenchuganj area, the Super Intendent of the Police and the General Manager of the Pakistan Industrial Corporation at Fenchuganj*".

I thought to myself there must be that person who gave the order to the police to beat the public to get down from the Train roof. I hurried to change my clothes to look like an ordinary man and started serving the guests present. When I was out of the door, one of them asked my father, '*Who was the Gentleman who served us food on the dining table?*".

My father replied "*Why, he was my Eldest son who just came from Sylhet by Train*". The SDO at once recognised me, he told my father the story in the Sylhet railway station and had said "*He really has got Guts!*" he exclaimed.

"*He was the one who ordered the Police to stop and also threatened me, if I had not stopped it, there would be a massacre at the railway station!*".

He told my father that I had stopped the commotion and eased the situation at the station. He asked my father "*Are all your sons the same?*" and my father replied "*Yes, they are all more or less the same!*".

When I returned to the room he thanked me for thinking of the welfare and of the people and controlling the situation.

PURAN BAZAAR

At that time preparations were being made for the annual sports of Puran Bazaar High School and I was invited as Chief Guest to attend the ceremony. I could not refuse. It was a remarkable event, not only the parents were invited by the school, the top civil servants, the police officers, and the village Head, including the Chairman of the Union Council. The school was founded by my father who donated the land, the playground etc and was also the Chairman of the Union Council. After the death of my father years later, my younger brother an Ex-Army Officer was the Chairman of the Governing Body. At that time I happened to be in Bangladesh about to return to England.

The annual sports started as a grand event. At the end there was a long run between the guests present and the teaching staff. A lot of people who knew me requested me to participate in the long run. I politely refused but it was of no use, I simply had to participate with the others. I said to myself, I know I would run faster than everyone else but would get tired at the end and slow down and lose the race.

No-one listened to my protests and indeed this is what happened. I ran really fast and was ahead of everyone but while I reached the middle of the field my ankle on the left side was severely hurt. I could not move my foot and fell on the ground. People came running to help me stand on my feet but I could not.

Later on, they carried me to my brother's house opposite the sports ground. The Doctor came and visited me. The porters from the nearby tea garden also came and applied some herbal medication on my leg. I was slightly relieved. The next day I had a flight to Dhaka. I came to my sister's house. I had vigorous pain. I met her son in law who was a pharmacist in Dhaka. He was adamant that I should go to a highly qualified doctor with foreign degrees. I went reluctantly to visit him. He gave me a long list of prescriptions and asked me to have a blood test and an x-ray of my foot. I thought it was bogus! I would never follow his advice nor was I going to spend money and time for nothing!

After coming back to my sister's house, I asked my brother in law if there was any homeopathy practitioner. He told me there was a colleague of his who practises free to the rikshaw drivers. He sits in his chamber under a

shed by the road side in a derelict area of Mog Bazaar I would love to see him. I believed in the benefits of homeopathy as my father used to treat us with such remedies when we were children. We did end up visiting him and he was surprised to see us. I told him how I became injured and he listened intently. He gave me three doses of medicine and told me one doze for now, one tomorrow morning and the final one in the evening. He told me that God willing I would sleep well and the next morning I would be able to catch my flight. I did exactly as he instructed and arrived at Heathrow safe and sound. I returned to Bangladesh some eight months later.

POLITICAL UPHEAVAL

The end of 1971 was a very crucial political upheaval in East Pakistan. The Government of Pakistan had refused Bengali language to be recognised alongside with Urdu as a state language of Pakistan in 1952. Bengalis were basically rice eaters, the price of rice went higher and higher, sometimes beyond the capacity of the affordability of ordinary people. Clothes, gold, and other commodities were very expensive. Bengalis started eating chapatis (national food of West Pakistan), there again started the discrimination in employment in full scale. Well educated people of East Pakistan were deprived of being employed in executive jobs in civil service, railways, military and other public services.

They started saying, *'Is that why we wanted independence in 1947?'*.

They raised their voice against the ruling authorities at this critical juncture, Sheikh Mujibur Rahman emerged. He, having stood in the election won the majority votes.

But Zulfiqar Ali Bhuto had said *'How can a Bengali be the Prime Minister of Pakistan?'*. Bhuto took the seat of Prime Minister himself despite the Bengalis being the majority population of Pakistan at that time.

Sheikh Mujibur Rahman then started mobilising the Bengali people and demanded provincial autonomy in East Pakistan. But the government flatly refused, instead deposed the governor of East Pakistan who was a Bengali person, and appointed a brutal military general as governor who used to undermine and underestimate Bengali people while he was in military service.

He found that the Bengalis were intelligent, artful and tactful and thoughtful. He took the control of the radio station and announced that he is not a weak-minded lenient person. He even referred to himself on the radio as a *'Brutal, cruel, human being'* who could do what he wanted to do. His name was Tikka Khan. He knew how to deal with the insurgents in East Pakistan. Bengali people were not dissuaded by the mere threats of this nature. He ordered first to get rid of the intelligentsia of the Bengalis.

THE FIGHT FOR INDEPENDENCE

The army raided houses at the odd hours of the night, killed all high ranking Bangladeshi Officers and service holders mercilessly in front of their wives and children. They raided the shops, social areas, cinema halls, streets, and targeted all sorts of public gatherings wherever they identified Bengalis. However the people were not frightened by these threats and they were determined for the independence of the east wing of Pakistan.

Sheikh Mujibur Rahman became the Leader, later known as *'Father of the Nation'* and took the initiative to strive for independence.

One particular day, I witnessed a cruel sight in front of me. People were coming out of their early morning prayers and the army began shooting those identified as Bengali people flat on the streets!

This cruel atrocity was being conducted all over East Pakistan at the same time of the Fajr Prayer.

In some villages, they called the villagers, the school teachers, doctors and others in a row and shot them all. We all became fearful for our lives. People got scared and fled from their houses to wherever they could find shelter. The fire was random, killing intellectuals and villagers, randomly. Shops were closed, open markets selling rice, fish, vegetables and food stopped functioning completely. People were in distress. Hindus were identified as enemies. Their lives were at stake. The army thought that people both Hindus and Muslims were their enemies. The Muslims of East Pakistan joined the Hindus as friends who were helping them morally and physically. They believed the Bengali's were basically Hindus (sharing the same national dress – the Sari) and the army wanted them to go back to India. The Bengalis, 80% of whom were Muslims, fled from the country through hills and jungles where the army could not reach. India sheltered them all, some young and middle aged people started undertaking military training in India.

They were called The Liberation Army of East Pakistan, later known as Bangladesh. There were Indian trained Generals who were disregarded and not utilised in Pakistan because they were Bengali. Having had all the training and ability to serve, they formed the liberation army.

After receiving the full training they came back to East Pakistan. They demanded the independence of East Pakistan, to be called Bangladesh. The Pakistani Army surrendered to the combined forces. Their soldiers either surrendered, were killed, or arrested, by the allied forces of East Pakistan and India through the execution of the liberation army. Sheikh Mujibur Rahman took the lead, he had demanded three things: (1) the language movement – Bengali to be recognised alongside Urdu as the national language of Pakistan, (2) Provincial autonomy – each province to manage their own affairs, and (3) for Bangladesh to be recognised as an independent state. He was taken to prison because he had been voted for President with the majority vote by the population of Pakistan. He was taken imprisoned in Pakistan for political reasons. Later he was released. When he visited England, he had a warm welcome from the Bangladeshis living in England. He had the full support of the British government ministers and other political parties who supported the cause of Bangladesh to become an independent country.

FLEEING TO SAFETY

In 1971 we were living in Sylhet. The fighting was still continuing and we were living in fear of the Pakistani Army. We had to leave our house and go back to our village home. Where some other families took shelter including my wife's parents. The army used to visit our village to find the trace of the Liberation Army who were fighting against the Pakistan Army.

One day my father and myself with some other people were sitting outside the mosque on a bench. We found many tea garden labourers running fast from the Lakatora (The Tea State) to unknown destinations towards the hilly area outside our village.

My father asked them, "Why are you running like this?"

They replied, that they were the workers of Lakatora Tea State and their Manager had been shot dead. The army had taken over the tea garden. They were looking for the Liberation Army who were fighting for independence and destroying everything in their path.

The Army had shot the Manager of the Tea State along with other office staff, the remainder were fleeing for their lives with family and children. The army could come to our village at any time and my father thought this would be a disgrace if they searched our house and we feared for our lives.

At our house, Jitu's wife English Alice who was living with us with two children. They were British citizens of the UK. Rumour spread that the British citizens might be collaborators of the British Army, the supporters of the Independence movement in Bangladesh. We might be shot as well. My father told me we should go back to

England as I was also a British Citizen by then and take Alice and her children back to safety in the UK.

But we were facing another problem. Alice did not want to go back to England yet, she was enjoying learning the culture of Bangladesh! She stayed in Bangladesh for three years and had learned the Sylheti language, cooking and eating Bengali food and the way of life! She was wearing a Sari like traditional Bangladeshi women, she learned and practised the culture quite well and made friends with other women in the village. She was loved by all around her. She enjoyed the open area of the village and swimming pool inside the boundary of our home.

She was really sad to leave as she had become fully accustomed to the lifestyle. She said that she did not want go back to live in a burdened, caged life. But she agreed to my father's wishes most reluctantly and returned to the UK.

SAVE THE ENEMY

At that time many more young Bangladeshis fled to India and joined the Guerrilla force named as the Liberation Army of Bangladesh. India opened its borders to the Bangladeshis. Many people fled to India to save their lives. The youth formed training centres, they were trained by the Indian Army in different camps to fight with the Pakistani Army. Mrs Indira Ghandi gave every support to the Bangladeshis to be trained to fight the Pakistani soldiers in Bangladesh to fight for independence.

The Bangladeshi Guerrilla force came back with the regular Indian Army and together they fought the Pakistani soldiers. The Pakistani Army gained control of some places and lost control of other places. The fight was going on almost everywhere. The situation was so uncertain. We were living in suspense, without knowing what would come next. Shooting, beating and killing continued everywhere.

The Army took control of Fenchuganj.

My father was informed that Mr Sajjad Ali Chowdhury has been arrested by the Pakistani Army. He was the secretary of Awami League, the party supporting the independence of Bangladesh. He would definitely be shot to death. He was one of the leaders of Muslim League, supporting the independence of India from the British rule in 1947 in congress, and now in 1971 he was supporting the independence of Bangladesh.

He was a colleague of my father, sitting as adjudicators on the bench while deciding disputes with the two rival groups in the village. My father, the Head of one group and Mr Sajjad Ali the Head of another group, who were enemies for generations with 49 pending land disputes and criminal cases against each other on land matters.

Once during a dispute between the rival parties, there was a bounty of 20,000.00 rupees placed on my father's head by the opposing party. If anyone could kill Firu Miah (the nickname of Delwar Hussain Chowdhury) he (Mr Sajjad Ali) would pay them this money. One day, My father was in the local market and someone came up to him and hit him on the head with a steel rod. He fell down and was seriously injured. The local market keepers and our tenants were enraged and loved my father a lot. We never charged them any rent and in return they would always protect us.

They began running and yelling. They caught the perpetrator and hit him mercilessly and he ended up in the hospital.

Even though there were so many disputes between my father and Sajjad Ali, my father appeared before the Major fearing that Sajjad Ali would be killed and asked for mercy.

He said to the Major, Mr Mughul Khan of the Pakistani Army

'If you have to kill him, kill me first, for he was the one who upheld the law, always. Let him go free!'.

At this the Major set him free.

He was released and came to our house at night. He simply could not believe that my father, his sworn enemy, would plead on his behalf to the Major risking his own life and was sincerely grateful.

He apologised to my father in front of a large gathering for what he and his family had done against our family for generations and many years. He openly declared the withdrawal of all pending false and fabricated cases against my father, and they shook hands.

The feud finally ended and with it came the end of animosity of two families.

However, the political situation remained the same, even worse than ever.

Although my father was a well-respected landowner, Chairman of the Union Council and an ex Muslim Leaguer, he could speak English very well and fluently. The Pakistani Army trusted him. Not a single villager was killed or persecuted in Noorpur within the Geographical area of Fenchuganj unlike other places, but nobody knew what might happen. The situation was uncertain in Bangladesh.

My father started to find air tickets for six of us. Myself, my wife and my son, and Alice and her two children to fly back to England sooner rather than later. The situation was getting worse and it was risky to stay.

RETURN HOME

When Alice agreed, we decided to leave and return back to England. But it was so risky to make the journey because we would have to travel through Karachi, the then capital of Pakistan and we were British citizens and possibly targets.

We were advised by many people even the travel agents to travel through India, which would take some days more, but it would be safer. They suggested we go through India by road and take a longer route, but I believed it to be riskier than flying from Dhaka to Karachi, Pakistan to get to the UK. We did not listen to the travel agent's advice and my father booked the tickets for us. After we arrived in Karachi, we had no problem whatsoever. We were taken to Midway hotel and stayed there overnight.

The next morning, we flew to London Heathrow, our destination safe and sound without any difficulties.

After our arrival we found the situation with the Bangladeshis very tense. There were long programmes on the television about the independence of Bangladesh. The Bangladeshis were awaiting eagerly for the independence. Our plan of settling down in Bangladesh was not successful. There is an old saying, man proposes, God deposes. That became true in our case.

SHEIKH MUJIBUR RAHMAN

Bangladeshis in the UK under the leadership of one Justice Syed Abu Chowdhury who came to England as a Visitor from Bangladesh, united the Bangladeshis in the UK under one banner as one nation, demanding independence of Bangladesh. Mr John Stonehouse MP and many other British Politicians joined the campaign for the independence of Bangladesh. During that time, Sheikh Mujibur Rahman having been released from the jail in Pakistan came to England. He mobilised the East Pakistani people (Bangladeshis) and demanded independence. At that time Bangladeshi Welfare Associations were formed in most towns and cities in the UK. Sheikh Mujibur Rahman held various meetings with Bangladeshis in London at Hyde Park and in other industrial cities with different community leaders. Their concern became a priority issue in the House of Parliament. Mr John Stonehouse MP and other parliamentarians directly supported the cause of the independence of Bangladesh. On 16th December 1971 Bangladesh was declared an independent country. The UK was the first country to recognise Bangladesh as an independent Country and the rest of the World gradually followed until it was on the World Map. It was Sheikh Mujibur Rahman, the Awmileague party which was the majority party which separated the country from Pakistan.

Sheikh Mujibur Rahman was the founder of the new Country of Bangladesh and he became the 'Father of the Nation' and had the title of Bhanga Bandhu, the friend of Bangladesh. Justice Abu Syed Chowdhury went to Bangladesh after Independence and became the first President of Bangladesh in 1971. After that the Father of the Nation Sheikh Mujibur Rahman took over the Presidentship of the Country but a few years after because of political reasons he was brutally murdered with some of his family members in Dhaka, except two of his daughters who were abroad. They were saved. Sheikh Hasina his daughter became the Prime Minister in later years. The Bangladeshi Army took over the country by a Coup. The political parties were banned. Later emerged another political party called Bangladesh National Party BNP under the headship of Ziaur Rahman, who was the former Army General. He died in a plane crash. His wife is Khaleda Zia later also became the Prime Minister at a different stage.

After some time Awamileague again came to power and Sheikh Mujibur Rahman's daughter Sheikh Hasina became the chair of the Awami Party and the Prime Minister. Khaleda Zia became the leader of the opposition.

When Bangladesh came into existence it had no expertise, not many experienced Teachers, Engineers, or government officers. The country had lost so many of its people in the fight for independence. Slowly it built up its infrastructure and is now one of the most progressive countries in the world.

RE-START

We re-started our lives in England. We were living in Bath and I looked into the best way to continue the maintenance of our family. I found that the restaurant was not making enough money to meet our financial needs although it was not a losing concern. My partner to whom I left the business with, employed a manager at a higher salary and my partner became a full-time student in Engineering. I did not want to be back in management of the business, I preferred to work elsewhere in industries.

I found a job with J S Fry Limited, Bristol. I started living with brother Jitu.

We found a house on Hanover Street, I paid the deposit and he obtained mortgage. I started work in the factory as a machine operator and we all lived together, Jitu, Alice, their two children, myself and my wife and my son Saadi. I worked in the manufacture of chocolates and worked the night shifts. Sometimes I used to work on a feeder machine, I had to lift various crates of unwrapped chocolates for wrapping. It was so heavy and the machine was too high to reach. It was really hard for me to work in this environment. Sometimes I used to work in the engine room which was very noisy and ear-piercing noises all through the night which was unbearable. Besides I had to change from one job to the other in the same factory. Coming from being the owner of a restaurant, from being the boss to following someone else's beck and call became so demeaning.

One morning when I came home after working on the night shift, I was told by Alice my brother's wife that I have been blessed with a beautiful baby daughter, Shakila. She was born in St Martin's Hospital in September 1971.

I had to travel to the hospital to see the baby and her mother but I had no transport. I bought an old Morris Minor car with £50 only which I could afford at that time and started using it on a regular basis for shopping, visiting the hospital and travelling to and from the factory. My wife never complained about the job I chose and always supported my decisions. She did not mind whether I was a manager of a restaurant or a factory worker and did not measure me with money. This was all the support I needed in life.

After around four months, I decided to return back to restaurant business and become my own boss again. I found a freehold empty premises ideal for a restaurant, exactly next door to the Odeon Cinema in Cheltenham, Gloucestershire. I managed to buy the freehold shop and converted it into a nice restaurant with a huge bank loan in 1972. Myself and my sister's husband Mr Malik were partners.

The premises had a four-bedroom living accommodation in the upper floors and we started to live there. There was a huge ground floor and cellar with a big garden. I converted it into a restaurant. It was a licensed restaurant serving Pakistani and continental food, at this time no one was aware of Bangladeshi food.

The Principal of North Gloucestershire College of Technology was the chief guest at the opening of the restaurant. The business was booming, customers used to dine even sitting on the staircase whilst there was no room to sit as the tables were fully booked. Well experienced staff were very hard to find at that time, Bangladeshi people were not prepared to travel to another town to work. They only wanted to work locally and be near their families., I had no option but to ask my eldest brother in law Mr Foysol who was studying for a Post Graduate Diploma in Management in London.

He was admitted into the North Gloucestershire College of Technology. Mr Foysol was almost heaven sent to help me. He studied and worked with me in the restaurant. He was my wife's eldest brother, who went on to settle in Canada where his family now reside.

At this restaurant, I had a troublesome Cook. He could not make rice in big portions using a big pot, nor was his food cooking any good. He could not make parathas and chapatis either! I had to call my wife from upstairs to come and cook those things. He could not even read the order in English! My wife had to come downstairs, leaving two babies; Shakila and another newly born baby, Sabina who were born only one year apart. It was extremely difficult to manage.

Sabina was a most beautiful baby, a little gem.

SALE OF THE CHELTENHAM BUSINESS

I became fed up and impatient. I did not want my wife to work in the restaurant kitchen at all. I decided to get rid of it even though the business was excellent. I put an advertisement in the Bengali Newspaper Surma for sale but it did not work. One day a friend of mine came on his day off and I started to tell him that I would like to sell the business. He showed so much interest in the business and told me that he tried to open a restaurant in Cheltenham for the past eight years but had failed. He told me that if I really wanted to sell it, he would buy it from me. I told him if he gave me his word; I would hand over the keys to him from tomorrow.

He agreed happily but it was sold with a cheap price. I lost a huge amount of money as I had to repay the loan. I had to also sell my partnership restaurant in Bath which was again a freehold business, but part owned by me.

Years ago, I had sold the freehold restaurant in Weston Supermare to the Lessee at a cheap price with no premium and payments would be made to me in monthly instalments. I incurred a heavy loss there too. There were too many staff problems and stresses in those businesses.

After selling my business I was walking aimlessly along the road and popped into the Job Centre in Cheltenham. I found an advert for Engineering Trainees. I was tested on Maths, General Knowledge and English. I passed them all and was selected for the traineeship in a Government Training Centre in Gloucester. Although I sold the restaurant verbally, I stayed in one of the rooms upstairs. The new owner did not allow me to stay outside or anywhere and wanted me to feel at home. He was an ex-employee of mine at the Taj Mahal Restaurant in Bath.

BIRMINGHAM

Every weekend I used to go to Birmingham to find a house to accommodate my family there. I found a house for sale and the man asked me if I wanted to view the house. I agreed and was shown around. It was quite a big house in Selly Park, in Birmingham but unmodernised. I agreed the price but I asked the seller if he would allow me and my family to live in the house before the completion of the purchase. His younger brother came along all of a sudden who objected, saying it would not be permissible to allow us in before completion of the purchase. There could be a problem later. Either I would not buy the house as promised or refuse to vacate the house. The elder brother was the owner of the house so he agreed to give me possession even though his younger brother had objected.

He said, 'Yes I would like to trust Mr Chowdhury, who would be morally responsible to me'.

He also agreed to hand over the key on the following Sunday. On that day I got ready, and I came alone with a suitcase only to find out if he kept his word. I found him standing outside the door waiting for me to hand over the keys. He gave me the keys as promised, his brother still would not agree. He had told him that although I was not known to him, I looked like a gentleman and trustworthy. He believed that I would not betray him. I assured him that I would pay rent at the market rate if in case I failed to buy the property.

The next day I brought my family from Cheltenham and moved into the house. At the end, as promised I bought the house on Hobson Road for £5,200.00 for a freehold property. I offered him rent but he would not accept any. I was so grateful to him. Later on he became a close friend of mine and his younger brother started calling me a 'Brother'.

FACTORY LIFE

By that time I finished my engineering training. My first job was in Lucas Engineering as a Capstan Operator. I worked there for some time in the Factory in Spring Road in Tyseley Birmingham which is now a Housing Development. Then I moved to a Precision Engineering company with a better pay scale, and then on to two other companies.

I was working at another factory. It was the month of Ramadhan and I had been fasting all day. At sunset I broke my fast for only five minutes. When I finished, the Foreman came and rudely told me off for not working. He asked If I consider my job as a joke. He said this was a work place and not a time for leisure. I told him I had permission from the Production Manager who knew about it. Still he didn't listen to me. I lost my temper and took my white coat off and I went home, leaving the job behind. I had my salary sent home by post at the end of the week.

I got a job working at WS Precision Engineering company as a Quality Control Inspector and then with Parker Hales Ltd, a gun Manufacturing Company.

One day I met a friend who had been with me in Bristol, he told me there was a Chinese takeaway for sale. I said I was looking to buy a takeaway. I agreed to buy but I did not know anything about Chinese cuisine, nor did I have any experience of how to cook it. Above all I did not have sufficient funds to convert it into an Indian takeaway. The owner agreed to train us in Chinese cooking, both the husband and wife used to come every night to train myself, my wife and my brother in law Forhad during opening hours and taught us how to cook all the menu items. We also employed another person who started to get the training for about three months.

221

I continued my employment with Parker Hales Ltd, I used to work at 8am at the factory until 4:30pm. At the same time my wife began working at Cadbury's chocolate factory during the day time. We then worked in the takeaway in the evening together in the Chinese takeaway to pay our debts. Customers kept asking me how did I know how to prepare Chinese food if I wasn't Chinese. Our financial condition was extremely bad at the time so both my wife and myself decorated the takeaway ourselves. I made a new counter top by hand and we painted the shop as we could not afford to engage a builder for the job.

It was too hard for me to run the business and work in the factory. As the opening time of the takeaway business was at 5pm until midnight. In addition I had to drop my chef home by car after closing time. I used to get to bed at 1:30am and get up for work at 6:30am at the latest. We also had a school run to do. Both my wife and I were doing this.

We carried on working both jobs and at the takeaway. Eventually, we bought the business from the owners with our savings that we had kept underneath our wardrobe.

One day a distant relative of mine came and saw me struggling like this. He gave me ideas and offered me some money to convert it into an Indian takeaway and put up a new sign. I had the signboard changed from Shampan Chinese Takeaway to Indian Food Centre and had the refurbishment done in an Indian style. I also changed the menu and decoration. Things started to turn around after it changed to south Indian cuisine as we had more experience in the food.

EMERGENCY

In 1977 my father had a serious heart attack and I wanted to go to Bangladesh with my cousin, my father's sister's son; Shamsu Bhai. I left the business in the hands of my brother in law Forhad, and my wife. Forhad was a student at the time. He was clever and efficient, the business would be in good hands. I left for Bangladesh, having reached there I found my father was lying in a hospital bed with his eyes closed. Suddenly his eyes opened and he saw us two standing by his bed. He was very surprised and asked why we were there all of a sudden.

He said *'Why did you come, I am not dying yet!'* He decided to leave the hospital and come and stay with us at our village home in Fenchuganj. One day my father and I were sitting under the dome of our pond (Fukri) in front of our house. A lot of people came to greet him, people passing through the road asked him with a loud voice from the other side of the pond,

"Are you well enough to be home?" they yelled over the distance. They all came to see him.

He asked me if I wanted to see the flying fish from the pond. He told me he would ask the fishermen to come with the net and catch the fish. He said to me that I would enjoy seeing the fish trapped in the net, the big breams would start flying and jumping inside the net. He really missed doing this with me and he knew that I missed it too. We both sat and watch the moving water in such peace and tranquillity, the trees swaying in the wind. The big fish were taken out from the net for dinner and the little ones thrown back in pond to grow bigger. I was surprised to see he was so excited to be watching the fish with me after many years, as if he was watching the World Cup!

Before being ill my father had planned to come and visit us in England. He wanted to stay with us for a few months and then return back home, stopping on the way back for a pilgrimage in Mecca (Hajj). He already got his passport and visa ready for the travel. He had his suitcase packed by my mother. My father asked me to check the suitcase as to whether the clothes were suitable to wear in a cold country like England. I looked at the clothes and I told him they were perfect for his trip.

One night he asked me,

"Why don't you go back to England to look after your new business?". I thought he must be right telling me to go back. So I retuned back to the UK thinking he would be coming to visit us soon.

After a month he sadly passed away. I have never stopped missing him.

He had a massive heart attack while adjudicating a dispute between two rival groups who were our tenants. The room was hot, he moved to my mother's room where there was a ceiling fan and was leaning down on a pillow and talking to the people. He was speaking aloud in the gathering which was usual for him , he was excited and his face turned pale. He said to the person sitting down near to him,

"Put a pillow under my head". He did it quickly and a moment later he told everyone:

"I am dying" and in the spur of the moment he left this world.

He died in front of all the people around him.

Inna Lillahi Wa Inna Ilayhi Rajioon – From God we come and to God we return.

I was so unfortunate that I left one month before his demise. I could not see my father or later my mother, at the time of both their deaths.

I was living in England whilst my younger two brothers Oyes and Koyes went on holiday to Singapore and then to Bangladesh went to see my parents, they had the opportunity to see both parents together while my sister from Dhaka came a month before his death to take care of him, she only left for a five minute walk to my sisters house and when she returned she found she had missed his last breath.

We lost our beloved father on the 10th August 1977. The light of Hasan Dynasty was out, along with the light of my life. it was an extremely difficult time and a shock for all of us.

MY SECOND SON

Back in the UK I continued to look after the business which had improved a lot. I was having a peaceful time for around three years or so. I bought a new property in Quinton and rented it out. I was approached by some members of the community to sort their problems, I got involved in community affairs in my spare time and almost as a tribute to my father's memory who had always helped the community. The business came into some difficulty. The chef had gone, my brother in law Forhad who used to help me a lot in running the business had to join an Accountancy firm for practical experience. We started living upstairs above the takeaway on Bearwood Road. I was lost and I could not find a proper chef and I was not used to working as a chef so I became determined to get rid of the business. I sold it in 1979. We moved to the house in Quinton and were expecting the birth of my second soon Raadi who was born in 1980.

We lived at our much loved home on Quinton Road West which gave us many years of wonderful memories which our extended family members also remember fondly. We rented this house out many times when we continued to move around. When I took my wife to hospital, she was overdue by four days. Then nurses joked that it must be a boy as he is taking too long to come into the world.

When he was born, I made a wish to God that would follows a spiritual and religious path in life. He did extremely well in school and at his college the teacher told me, he had never met a boy of such high intelligence. On one occasion I went to a mosque and heard someone giving the Azaan (Call to prayer) in such a beautiful voice that everyone wanted to know who it was. Someone informed me that it was actually my son!

After Raadi was born, my wife and I went to perform our holy pilgrimage (Hajj) in Mecca.

226

RELOCATION

In 1981 was financially hard up. I sent my family, my wife and three children to Bangladesh and put the house in Hobson Road for sale. Myself and my elder son Saadi stayed back. We decided to shift back to Bangladesh and my wife and children had moved in with her parents. My father in law was an Advocate in the District and Sessions Judges Court (Crown Court) in Sylhet and my mother in law was a retired secondary school teacher in a girl's high school. She used to teach Bengali to my two daughters and the little baby stayed with my wife.

They provided a sound environment for my family and my children began schooling in Bangladesh. It was very difficult for them as they were British children in a completely new country but they learn how to read, write and speak Bengali. Both had passed the admissions test in Government Girls Pilot High School, Sylhet. My eldest daughter reached 10 years old and obtained a scholarship.

In 1983 they came back when I was living in Bristol with my eldest son Saadi who was attending Cottam Grammar school for this GCEs. We lived above a takeaway in Bristol together but then moved to my brother's house with the family. The takeaway was my brother's in Bristol with the same name as my takeaway in Birmingham, Indian Food Centre. Our house in Quinton had been rented out. I was attending some courses at Bristol University for better job prospects.

We hurriedly bought a house in Cropthorne Road in Bristol with the help of my younger brother Oyes. We stayed at his house whilst the purchase was going through, we then moved to the house and my daughters started school in Bristol in Pen Park High School and my little son Raadi attended nursery school. As they had just returned from Bangladesh, Raadi came back from

Nursery school one day and asked me why the teachers could not speak Bengali!

SHIFA-E-KAMILA

My wife's brother Forhad and his wife came to live with us in Bristol and my wife was expecting our fifth child in 1984. I came from work one night and my wife had some pain. She told me I had to take her to the hospital and I said I was hungry so she fried me some samosas and waited patiently for me to finish them all the while in pain herself! I saw she was mixing the dough and rolling the samosas into shapes, and she was stopping to grip the counter in pain.

I told her to stop but she said if she dies in childbirth, she wants to make sure she makes my wishes come true first! So she picked up the oil canister and put it down again in pain. She just about managed to fry a few samosas and we had our last meal together before setting off for Southmead hospital where my daughter Kamila Haseen was born in March 1984. I wanted to choose her name specifically, because it means both knowledgeable and beautiful.

Now she is a Solicitor in Birmingham and my daily companion. If you put her name with my wife's it would be Shifa-e-Kamila meaning Complete Healing.

My wife's brother Forhad and his wife, Ruby lived with us. Ruby used to put Kamila to sleep and make her eat her dinner by creating little lumps of rice and telling her the story of 'Chicken Licken and the Sky is Falling Down'. They had a very close bond and Kamila really believed the sky was going to fall down!

MOVING BACK TO QUINTON

In 1986, the house in Birmingham was up for sale through estate agents. They said it would be sold quickly if it was left empty. We made the tenants leave for a quick sale and left all electrical equipment there, fridge freezer, washing machine etc. One day the agents telephoned me in Bristol to say that the house had been burgled. The equipment including the central heating boiler had been stolen! A stream of water had spread all over the ground floor from the disconnected boiler and pipes. Unless those things were repaired or replaced the prospective buyer would not proceed to buy the house. I became angry and said to the estate agents to tell the purchaser that I no longer wished to sell the house and withdrew it from the market. I would come back to live there.

Within two weeks we sold the house in Bristol and moved back to Quinton, Birmingham. I replaced all the equipment as necessary and started our lives here. The children were admitted in their respective schools and we did not move again after this. I did not have a job in Birmingham and I had plenty of time as such to resume my studies. This time in a practical manner studying in the public library in Birmingham on a regular basis for a few hours a day. I studied about the ethnic minorities groups in the UK and their social, economical and education needs and how to improve their lifestyles in correlation to other groups in the UK.

*

HAJJ FOR MY MOTHER

In early 1986 I was living in Quinton with my family. My mother asked me to perform Hajj (pilgrimage) on her behalf as she was old and frail and unable to undertake the journey to Mecca and Medina.

I went to Mecca and met some people whom I knew from Sandwell. They informed me that a new job for a Community Development Officer was going to be advertised in the newspaper. They wanted me to apply for the new post which they thought I would be well suited for on my return to Birmingham.

After performing the sacred act of Hajj for my mother, according to the tradition I went straight to see my mother at my village home in Bangladesh.

I then went to Sylhet to see my in-laws. The next day there was a TV forecast which showed a political upheaval. General Ershad, the Military chief of Bangladesh declared a coup which took over the Presidentship of Bangladesh. I had to return home to the UK as quickly as possible to avoid any other serious political problems. I went to Sylhet railway station to go home. But the train was so crowded with panic stricken passengers. There was no room to stand inside the compartments, but I managed to get on the train somehow. I remained standing the entire journey. I found a well dressed smart looking gentleman sitting down comfortably which his wife by his side. She was occupying double the space she required. I politely asked the gentleman if he would kindly move over a little so I could give some comfort to my aching feet as I had been on my feet for a long time. At this he got angry and said to me,

"Can't you see we are already squashed?!"

I said, "*I understand, but could you possibly move a little and give me some space to sit?*".

He got really angry and said "*No!*".

I told him, "*It doesn't matter, after the train crosses the outer signal, you will pull my hand and ask me to sit by your side*". He started laughing at me.

After the train crossed the outer signal and the gentleman finally said to me "*Brother, you can sit here. I can see you are so tired*".

I said "*No, No I am fine, don't worry about me! Its not too far to reach my destination. Its only fifteen miles to Fenchuganj*"

He then enquired, "*Are you from Fenchuganj*?" he did not believe me, as I was speaking with his Bengali dialect.

He asked me if I knew Mr Mahmud us Samad Chowdhury from Fenchuganj. He said that he was his brother in law. He asked me how far my house was from his.

I said, "*We live in the same house. He is my younger brother*".

We then started chatting and became friendly with one another. I told him I knew his Uncle Moulana Moslehuddin, who conducted my marriage ceremony.

He gave me a space to sit and apologised for not allowing me earlier. He then offered me paan and snacks very lovingly. His wife prepared the paan with Zarda (hot spice). He told me that we were related to each other.

By the train the train had arrived at Fenchuganj station he gave a salaam to me with a loud voice, and said "I wish we would have met before so we could have spent more time together!".

I returned to the UK.

THE MOST SUITABLE CANDIDATE

After a few weeks I saw an advertisement in the newspaper to appoint a mature Bangladeshi person who would be fluent in different dialects in Bangladesh and having knowledge speaking and understanding of Urdu and Punjabi to address the needs of the multicultural needs of the community in the Borough of Sandwell. It was identified by the House of Commons report published in 1986 that Bangladeshis' were the latest addition to the ethnic minority in the UK. They had a distinct cultural background, coming mostly from rural areas of Bangladesh. They needed help and support in housing, education, recreation, social integration, training for jobs, English language etc. They did not know where to seek support from. They were even unaware of their own basic welfare rights and benefits available to them. To address these, the Sandwell Metropolitan Borough Council advertised this post to appoint a Bangladeshi Development Officer.

I found it very interesting, this was the kind of job I was looking for to serve the community better and in my father's memory. I would be able to help the community in an organised and authorised manner. I was fully confident I could make a difference in the community. I applied for the job and was interviewed and tested in every possible way. There were so many candidates who applied for this job. Candidates came speaking different accents, from many education backgrounds, including a leader of the Council and an Officer from the Community Development Department of the Chief Executives in Sandwell. It included the Chief Racial Equality Officer of the Sandwell Borough Council.

I was successful and got the job as the first Bangladeshi Community Development Officer in the Borough of

Sandwell to work under the Umbrella of some fourteen Bangladeshi Organisations called Sandwell Confederation of Bangladeshi Muslims Organisations (SCOBMO).

As I was the first Officer appointed, there was no systematic trail, no clue or previous defined rules, no contact numbers of service providers, but had one identifiable target, to develop the under achieved Bangladeshi community in the Borough of Sandwell.

DEVELOPMENT MANAGER

The Project was initially approved for four years, funded jointly by the Department of Environment of Central Government, The Home Office, and by the Sandwell Metropolitan Borough Council. The local government's pay and conditions rule applied. After four years it became an ongoing project. The local governments pay and conditions committee composed of the council officers including the non statutory and non-voluntary organisations securitised all posts funded by the council, increased, decreased or retained the post holders job titles and salaries of all those appointed. As for me, the job title and the salaries were increased substantially to a higher grade as a principal officer. I was offered to be called The Development Manager or Director. I thought the word Director was a bit too flashy so My job title was changed to Development Manager moving up from Development Officer.

I carried on with my job as Development Manager. I was the only Development Manager who launched campaigns against the decision makers. I was attached to many more Management Committees, both in statutory and non-statutory organisations. Namely Racial Harassment Unit, Equal Opportunities Policy and Practice, Recruitment and selection of Officers. I was involved in the consultation in 1997 of the Human Rights Act which came into force in 1998 as a statutory instrument. I was a member of the following committees: The Black Country Development Corporation, Council's Emergency Action Committee, Community Fund Allocation, Review of Council's Strategy Committee, Police Liaison Committee, Sandwell Training and Enterprise Council, Standing Advisory Committee for Religious Education in Sandwell, Sandwell College Ethnic Minority Advisory Committee,

236

Local Government Disciplinary Action Committee, Ethnic Minority Health Steering Group, Government Single Regeneration Budget in its economic theme group and many more.

RIVAL GROUPS

Life was not that easy, I was faced with a lot of incidents during my service period.

A rival Bangladeshi group who tried hard to stop the allocation of funding for the project and its Development Officer, I had to stand firm to protect the interest of the majority group of people of the Sandwell Confederation of Bangladeshi Muslims Organisation (SCOBMO) which was later renamed to be called 'CBO' (Confederation of Bangladeshi Organisations).

The rival group a small community group against SCOBMO was called The Bangladeshi Welfare Association who did not want to be part of the 14 Bangladeshi Organisations under one Umbrella. They wanted to be autonomous. They arranged a meeting in the Town Hall in Smethwick with the Council authority attended by the leader of the council, Councillor Ron Davis and Officers from the Department of Environmental Health and the Chief Racial Equality Officer of Sandwell. The leader of the opposition group arrogantly addressed Councillor Ron Davis, saying that the Development Officer appointed by the Local Authority was not doing anything for the community at all! He said that the tax payers money was going down the drain and that it must be stopped immediately!

Councillor Ron Davis in his reply said,

"So far as I know, from the Council's point of view, we have appointed the right person for the post. We know that the money is not being wasted. It was properly utilised for the benefit of the community and we as a council were aware of his success. The work of the Development Manager has appeared in the local press in

238

newspapers, the Sandwell express, the Evening Mail and others".

Ron Davis said, *"The work of the Development Manager was well appreciated"* and he told the opposition *"To have patience to appreciate the success".*

The meeting was a failure and the opposition group dispersed. Coming out from the Town Hall, the Chairman of SCOBMO Mr Uddin blamed me for not replying to the accusations. I said the Council Chief had already replied on my behalf and besides, I did not want to have a row with the opposition and lose my respect. I learned the method of response from my Father long ago.

In retaliation to this humiliation, the rival group held an election themselves illegally before the election of the Confederation and elected their office bearers, they then served me a notice to report to their Chairman for discharging my duties under them, being the intruders! I did not answer to this. They approached the Council to stop the funding for SCOMBO and wanted to slot in above us so we report to them. They sent me a letter to fire me. I did not care. I knew they were intruders and a group of crooks! I was appointed by the Council for SCOBMO; they had no right to discharge me as they were not my employers.

They went to the Council's Chief Executive who dismissed their unfounded and baseless claims. Then the group approached the Race Relations Unit to attend a meeting and air their complaints against SCOMBO and its Development Manager. I was invited to the meeting and I attended as the Development Manager for SCOBMO as it was a meeting of community affairs and related to the Bangladeshi Community.

They raised many issues against the Council, SCOBMO and the Bangladeshi Development Officer. One of their leaders, Mr Jagirdar gave a hot and aggressive speech which lasted for one and a half hours! At the end of the speech the secretary of the association, asked the Principal Race Relations Officer, Mr Zaidi to ask me to translate the whole lecture in Bengali.

I interpreted the whole lecture thoroughly and accurately without missing any point whatsoever. They were so surprised their mouths were open! They did not expect me to remember each point of their complaints so accurately.

At the end of the meeting their secretary ran to me from behind and had said,

"Mr Chowdhury, you told me once that you did not remember a lot of things that happen. How did you remember the whole lecture without missing a single point?"

I said, *"It was simply a blessing from God, nothing else"*.

He said, *"We planned to ask you to translate the whole lecture which you would never be able to do correctly and precisely as it was for such a long length of time, we wanted to prove your inefficiency for the post! But we could not"*.

The Race Relations Officer asked them, do you have any more questions? They replied, *"He is just super!"*.

MAINTAINING THE PEACE

In November 1988, we at Scobmo held our Annual General Meeting. The rival group brought two coaches loaded with Bangladeshi people from other towns with the intent to create an obstruction during our election.

The insurgents surrounded our election venue in Smethwick, Birmingham and started a demonstration against Scobmo. The Chief Superintendent of the Police was in attendance, he called the Police and three or four vehicles arrived on the spot with uniformed officers. The rowdy elements then dispersed. They failed this time also. We managed to continue with our AGM undisturbed and many joined us later to have the benefit from our community programme. SCOBMO survived since 1986 as an outstanding Umbrella organisation for the Bangladeshi people in the borough of Sandwell and still exists today as CBO.

There were some external problems concerning the Muslims all over the world including the United Kingdom. Being a responsible person from the Confederation of Bangladeshi Muslims had to face with maintaining peace within the Bangladeshi community in the borough. It was in 1988 Salman Rushdie published a book called the Satanic Verses which was an insult to the Prophet Muhammad (A.S) and our religion. Muslims all over the world protested against this book which was a direct controversy to our religious book which we refer to as Quranic verses.

Muslims were outraged. There were mass demonstrations in London and gathered in a protest rally demanding the withdrawal of such an insulting book from the market. Even the life of Salman Rushdie had been threatened by many. In 1989 Ayatollah Ruhollah

Khomeini of Iran passed a Fatwa against Rushdie for Blasphemy. A coachload of Muslims from SCOBMO joined the mass demonstration. As a result, the police, the Council of Muslims, community relations, multifaith groups and all religious groups joined in Sandwell Council House came together and urged the Muslims to calm down and maintain the peace. It was broadcasted on the BBC News.

After all the situation was brought under control. Salman Rushdie was hiding somewhere on police protection as the news spread.

GANG WAR FARE

In December 1992 at Audhya Uttar Pradesh in India the Hindu Nationalist party, BJP, demolished the Barbari Mosque in Delhi, built by Babar the first Moghul Emperor in India in the year 1528-29.

The Mosque was one of the most illustrious buildings, a remarkable piece of Muslim architecture in India. The Hindu Nationalist Party claimed that it was built by Lord Rama himself on the hill of Rama. It had been occupied and demolished by BJP. There was a huge demonstration which resulted in riots between the Hindus and Muslims in India.

Many people lost their lives, many were injured and died. The news spread throughout the world. Immediately after that the Muslims all over the World raised their voice in protest in the UK the Muslims became angry and agitated. They burned some Hindu Temples and caused damage as such. The Hindus did the same back to Muslims. The police, members of the community, and all related communities, held meetings and urged both Hindu and Muslims to ease the situation and maintain peace.

The programme was also televised on the National News. Mr Siddhu, The Chief Racial Equality Officer from Sandwell MBC and myself representing SCOBMO and other community organisations appeared before the BBC appealing to the public to maintain the peace and not take the law into their own hands. We promoted peace and harmony between community groups.

LIST OF ACTIVITIES

During my time in SCOBMO I was involved in the following:

- Supply of quality Halal food to Muslim patients in hospitals
- Introduction of Halal food to the Meals on Wheels elderly community
- To improve the interpretation services at GP Surgeries, Court of Law and Hospitals where there was a requirement for Sylheti speaking Interpreters. The current Interpreters spoke Bengali where 95% of the Bangladeshi people in the Borough spoke Sylheti.
- Appointment of Bangladeshi people in social services, hospital services, and various NHS bases. To employ and train people where unqualified Bangladeshi people where appointed for training to become qualified social services workers.
- Obtain permission from the Ministry to increase the volume of Halal Poultry in grocery shops. There was only a limited number of Halal chickens in abattoirs and I had to approach the Ministry to increase the quota.
- Arranged separate timings for male and females in swimming pools to provide more facilities to Muslim women were necessary. To maintain cultural requirements and identity.
- Extended the provision of ESOL (English for speakers of other languages) for immigrants were necessary for those who could not speak English.
- Bangladeshi men were working in catering establishments mostly or as labourers in industries as they were speakers of Bengali

244

- language only. They were encouraged to undergo trainings in government training centres to find more opportunities for employment elsewhere.
- Some Bangladeshi's who were graduates or even post graduates could not find proper venues to develop themselves, they were advised to undergo further training in educational institutes to have requisite qualifications in teaching profession.
- Along with the Army and civil service recruiting team I visited the Gurdwaras, temples, mosques and Islamic centres encouraging the ethnic minorities to get into those services where their religious and cultural practices are recognized.
- To develop and support recreational activities within the community to celebrate cultural diversity using events and activities. Such as, cultural events, Independence Day of Bangladesh, international language day, birthday of the father of the nation, organising football teams, obtaining funding for uniforms for players and pitch hire with the funding obtained from the local council. Furthermore, establishment of mosques and Islamic centres in some parts of Sandwell and develop cultural activities, hobbies and interests for the community. In one of these events my youngest daughter sang a wonderful religious song.
- The Institute of Bilingual studies had a shortage of DPSI qualified interpreters. Bangladeshi educated people were encouraged to enrol on the DPSI course to become official interpreters with the Statutory and Public Service Interpretations.
- Child Bride cases, a number of young girls were taken to Bangladesh, India and Pakistan for

forced marriage. I was involved in supporting the families and individuals and reducing the overall number of occurrences which was drastically removed. There was a young girl who ran away from home in fear of forced marriage. I was asked to speak with the girl and liaise with the family to ensure a peaceful outcome and the treat of forced marriage was removed. I became an emotional support for the families and the youths in my community and united many families in the process.

- SCOBMO advice and information centre with its trained staff provided services to 2500-3000 clients every year on Welfare Rights, Housing, Employment, Immigration and Nationality and has been gaining a financial support to the extent of £1,358,900.00 for local residents in the metropolitan borough of Sandwell in one year alone.
- The advice and information centre of SCOMBO received accreditation from the Office of the Immigration Services Commissioner OISC.

PERSONAL ACHIEVEMENTS

During the period of my service at SCOBMO, I was elected a representative of Sandwell's 17,000 ethnic minorities to the government's single regeneration budget in its economic regeneration Theme Group to allocate funding to improve rundown industrial and manufacturing premises which were already shutdown in the Borough of Sandwell.

I had been an examiner of the Institute of Bilingual Studies in its Diploma in Public Service Interpretation (DPSI). Under the rules introduced on that time on the DPSI qualified interpreters would be appointed in the course of law public and private services as qualified interpreters, not their friends, children or relatives having no such qualification.

I was a member of The Institute of Welfare Offices (MIWO 1988). A member of the Chartered Management Institute (MCMI 1990). A member of the Commonwealth Magistrate and Judges Association (CMJA 1994). A member of the Magistrates association, UK (1993).

I also appeared in Asian *"Who's Who"* international on its publication in 2003. (Published by Asian Observer Publications UK Page 77).

I was featured in the book named *"Britain e Bangladeshi (Bangladeshis in Britain)"*, published by centre for information and research Sylhet, in its first edition November 1999 (Page 607).

In 1992 I became the Justice of the Peace in Birmingham West Midlands, the first Bangladeshi to be appointed as J.P.

I was involved in 49 organisations and committees including, the Standing Advisory Committee on Religious Education in Sandwell, Sandwell College Ethnic Minorities Ethnic Minorities Committee, Co-opted School Governor of Churchfield High School in West Bromwich, Sandwell Training and Enterprise Council, The Black Country Housing Development Corporation, The Institute of Bilingual Studies and many more voluntary organisations.

I received a Lifetime Award from Sandwell Confederation of Bangladeshi Organisations.

JUSTICE OF PEACE

Before sitting on the bench as a Justice of Peace, I had to take two oaths, the Oath of Allegiance, and the Judicial Oaths. I sat at the Magistrates court dealing with criminal cases.

When I was young, in Bangladesh, I used to attend courts of the magistrates, district judges and the high court accompanied by my father. We had multifarious cases, especially on land matters. My father in law was an Advocate who practised in Dhaka High court and one of his cousins was the Chief Justice of Bangladesh, Sayed A. B. Mahmud Hossain.

After becoming a magistrate, I was not scared or hesitant to sit on the bench to adjudicate cases. It was indeed a responsible judicial task.

I enjoyed most of it as it was quite different from the routine and monotonous work. The cases were different from one another, and sentencing were different to each other as well. We were hearing cases of all sorts, burglaries, theft, casing actual bodily harm, abusive behaviour, affray, driving offences all sorts, aggravated vehicle taking, assault, breach of peace, criminal damage, cruelty to children, deception, drunkenness and disorderly behaviour, forgery, violent disorder and many more.

Sometimes I found a serious problem in decision making when sentencing. The law clearly says that, "the prosecution must prove the case beyond rescannable doubt". While in some cases, the prosecution failed to prove the case beyond the reasonable doubt, but we have to abide by the law, which could be against our conscience.

In that case we could seek advice from the legal advisors, if or when required on point of law. The legal adviser is either a barrister or a long-standing experienced solicitor known as the clerk to the Justices. Who would point out the law only, but it was the Justices to make the decision within the bounds of law.

I must mention one good thing which impressed me the most, was that I found no sign of racial or any kind of discrimination between the Justices on the bench or towards the accused. The concept of law and equality and human rights were ensured in all cases.

HEART ATTACK

In 2002, I had a serious heart problem.

I was having chest pain very frequently in the office, outside and at home.

I was sent to hospital where the specialist recommended an angioplasty procedure would be necessary. When taken for it, the surgeon did not want to go ahead with the procedure as the arteries were seriously damaged. So I was taken back to the waiting room where my family was waiting to hear the result.

They were surprised to see me back so soon. The surgeon explained that I needed a heart bypass operation instead immediately. My arteries were seriously damaged. The NHS waiting list was full and it would take a few months to wait for the operation date. My family thought NHS operation would take a few months to wait which could be too late for me. My family decided to have the operation done privately and quickly. The operation as such was done privately at Priory Hospital in Birmingham on the second day of September 2002. It was done successfully. My wife was provided a bed in my room in hospital. I was released after 12 days. And after 3 months, I was quite fit physically to get back to the office.

The sad part of the story was that I had to lose two of my younger brothers, Aziz us Samad Chowdhury a Business man in Bath and Wahid us Samad Chowdhury, the Deputy Mayor of the City of Bath. Both brothers died of heart attack just like my father. Their bodies were sent to Bangladesh and have been buried in our ancestral grave yard near to my father's grave.

PAAN CHEWING

Bangladeshi people are inclined to Paan chewing as a habit, this is a hard beetle nut (supari) with a special leaf called Paan. It is eaten with some paste and dried tobacco leaves called Zardah. It has a distinct, minty smell when eaten. It can stain your teeth and make them red. Whilst it is enjoyable, it is a bad habit. All these items are available to purchase in Bangladeshi grocery shops. Most people like to eat these after food or when sitting outside with their friends having a good time. It is also used as a refreshment to entertain guests

During my time working at SCOBMO, we had some Paan tested in a laboratory to check if there were any long term side effects of consuming the products.

It was revealed that this habit of Paan chewing could cause mouth ulcers and cancer!

The health authority were in touch with me on help and advice on how to spread in the community to dissuade people from this historical habit.

I held some community talks and had to appear in a video to raise awareness for the Bangladeshi community to inform them of the health concerns and bad affects of Paan chewing.

But people were reluctant to listen to the message as they simply loved Paan! Unfortunately, it is still regularly chewed by a lot of people, despite my best efforts.

MULTICULTURAL EVENTS

Every year. I organised cultural functions within the Metropolitan area of Sandwell with funding from the Council.

We would have live singing, dancing and talent contests. I would organise the food, guests, itinerary and market the event. We did this for many celebrations which brought together the community as one and all religions and cultures were celebrated with bright colours, clothing and world foods. It was a way to bring communities together and raise cultural awareness.

These events were attended by officers from different departments of the government, health, housing, education, the police force and the general public.

Poets, writers, singers, from all over the UK displayed their multi-talents for all to take part and enjoy the occasion.

On one occasion, the main group of singers from London were late as they were stuck on the motorway.

It had almost been an hour and the audience were restless. The Hall was full of people and chaos endued. What should have been a joyous event became a noisy gallery.

I had to bring some sort of control to the situation so I went onto the stage began telling some of my life stories to engage the audience. Everyone fell silent.

I told the audience, *"I am not a singer, but I can sing a little"*

I decided to throw caution to the wind, took one gulp of air and started singing a song 'Kando Kene Mon'. It was a song by a sentimental artist, Abbas Uddin Ahmed, a Folk singer from Bangladesh.

The audience were overwhelmed they screamed in joy, clapping their hands. They recognised the song and the words were bitter sweet. It evoked a huge amount of emotion in their hearts. The community simply could not envisage me that way, as I usually sat behind a desk in the office. By the time the real entertainers arrived at the event the audience were joyous and energised!

MY QURANIC STUDIES

During my childhood, I moved around many times and would stop and start with a new Arabic teacher each time. At one point I thought I would never be able to complete my reading of the Quran as I had become an adult and still not finished.

Muslims try to read the book of God in Arabic where possible and it was a desire of mine to be able to do this. As I had to keep restarting whenever I had a new teacher, I never managed to complete the whole Quran in my childhood.

In 1986 when I was employed as a Development Officer in Sandwell, I decided to pursue this.

I started reading the Quran on my own, I would check my reading with the Moulana at the mosque. It took me many years and I finally finished all 30 chapters of the Quran and became fluent in reading. I started reading different books written by scholars on Islam and instructions on how to read correctly. I made it a practice to read the Quran everyday which I still continue to this day.

It was very hard to find a teacher for my children, so I decided to teach them myself in the weekends and school holidays I also travelled to different homes to teach other children.

I was approached by one lady to ask if I would teach her son and daughter and she would pay me for this. I told her to send her children to my house and I would teach them with my own children, for free.

I did not want to take and money for this she was so pleased and honoured. Her children can now read the Quran fluently.

BANGLADESH AND ITS BEAUTY

Bangladesh itself is a most beautiful country. Miles upon miles of open lands, fresh air, swaying trees and beautiful lakes and rivers. It is a scenic place.

The country is known internationally for its produce and industry. They provide clothing to Marks and Spencer's, Primark, BHS, TESCO and many UK companies. Their IMPORT-EXPORT market is huge across the globe.

There are more than 160 tea gardens in Sylhet alone. Bangladesh is known for its famous tea. The 'Tea Capital' is Srimangal where there are many tea fields. You can see the tea workers in between the plants with their huge circular hats. There is even a famous, seven layer tea that must be tried!

There are fields of orange gardens in Beani Bazaar, where visitors can eat as many oranges as they wish whilst walking through the gardens.

There are rubber plants, trees and wood of every kind which are used to make furniture and incense sticks, tobacco leaves, and perfumes are created from the musk plants.

There are sugar cane fields and many fruit trees of pineapple, banana, mango, starfruit, jackfruit, lychees and so many more.

In Dhaka, there is a palatial building built in 1872. The palace of the Nawab is called 'Ahsan Manzil' is now a museum and a must see for tourists. The building is situated in Kumartoli along the banks of the Buriganga river in Dhaka. There is a Dome in the middle of the Palace and the exterior is a prominent pinkish colour which can be seen for miles. It is an architectural treasure.

In its glory days the Nawabs of Dhaka used to conduct their court affairs at this palace.

There is another prominent place, the Palace of Nawab Ali Amjad Pritim Pasha in Kulaura. This was a royal house of nobility. In 1895 the Clock Tower of Sylhet was constructed by the Nawab and presented by his father. It is still functioning today.

The city of Chittagang is home to Cox's Bazar. The longest uninterrupted sea beach in the world with an unbroken length of 155 kilometres! There are hotels, resorts, water sports and plenty of activities to do there. It is also a Navy sea Port and home to Himchari National Park which is a tropical rainforest. Also in Chittagang is Sheikh Mujib Safari Park. It spans over 2000 acres of land and contains an animal sanctuary. There is also an aquarium and a Marine Drive.

In 2017 hundreds of thousands of Rohingya refugees arrived in Cox's Bazar from Mynamar and Kutupalang became the largest refugee camp in the world.

Hazrat Shah Jalal was the much loved Sufi Saint in Bangladesh. He was educated in Mecca and received *Kamaliyat* (spiritual perfection) after 30 years of learning and meditation.

Writing of Hazrat Shah Jalal in his travelogue, the Rihla (The Journey) Ibn Battuta says:

'he was numbered among the principal saints, and was one of the most singular of men. He had done many noteworthy acts, and wrought many celebrated miracles. He used to remain standing (in prayer) all night. The inhabitants of these mountains received Islam from his hands, and it was for this reason that he stayed among them.'

The exact date of his death is debated but it was around 1346. He was buried in Sylhet in a tomb which is located in Dargah Mahalla. His shrine is famous throughout Bangladesh, with hundreds of thousands of tourists coming to visit.

Hazrat Shah Jalal's name is associated with the spread of Islam in Bangladesh. The largest airport in the country, Hazrat Shah Jalal International is named after him.

The Sundarbans Mangrove Forest covers an area of about 10,000 km2. There are three wildlife sanctuaries which were established in 1977 under the Bangladesh Wildlife (Preservation) (Amendment) Act, 1974. The Sundarbans constitute the world's largest contiguous mangrove forest which extends across India and Bangladesh.

RETIREMENT

I retired from my job on the 30th August, 2004 after 18 years of service in CBO. The Retirement party was a glorious farewell party. Many of the council officers including the Chief Racial Equality Officer, the police officers, chief of training enterprise council attended the party with Bangladeshis' in the borough of Sandwell.

A traditional lunch was arranged by CBO in a big hall. I had long service award from CBO. With load of expensive presents. The Bangladeshis' were pleased to have the invaluable service and achievement during the period of they had me as Development Manager.

I was delighted to hear when the leader of the council said in his speech that "*the Bangladeshis are well developed in Sandwell under the leadership of Mr. Z.S. Chowdhury*".

Immediately after my retirement I became free to travel where I wanted. My first choice was to visit the Taj Mahal in India where I went with my wife. She was been working for years as an Education Liaison Officer and Support Teacher to underachieving and special needs children. She also retired and we started a different time of our lives.

I had always wanted to move to a seaside town and live in a Bungalow near to the beach. I targeted Swansea where in my eldest daughter Shakila was living and employed as an Equality Officer with Swansea Council. We manged to buy a Bungalow not too far from the sea, near to my daughter's house who is now a practising Solicitor in Swansea.

We lived in Swansea for over 10 years. We felt somewhat lonely there. And there were no friends or relatives apart from my daughter's family.

We finally decided to move back to Birmingham, the city where we lived for over 35 years. I followed the tradition of the past, moving from one city to the other in my childhood with my uncle who used to be transferred in every two three years as an executive officer in civil service. In February 2019, we moved back to live in Birmingham to find our long-lost friends and our nearest relatives.

After my return back to Birmingham, I continued to have community involvement and became the Founder of Cambridge Solicitors LLP in Birmingham and Swansea. My two daughters continue my passion for the law as Solicitors, and follow my footsteps to provide services to assist the Bangladeshi Community in the UK.

My wife is the real partner of my life. We started working together in the garden since our retirement. I do the digging she does the planning, laying the seeds to grow some vegetables and flower plants. She also does the cooking and I do the idle gossiping by her side.

Our family life is happy and peaceful. We have five lovely children. The first one is Saadi who graduated in Public Administration in 1990, working as a Consultant, the second, a daughter Shakila obtained LLM and practicing as a Solicitor in Swansea. The third is a daughter, Sabina, after her law degree obtained a master's degree in Medical Ethics. She had been appointed as the Deputy Chief Officer within the Health Council in Birmingham. She now lives in USA and works as a Real Estate Agent. The fourth, a son, having an IT software business and fifth and the last one, a daughter Kamila, settled in Birmingham opened a Solicitor's firm called Cambridge Solicitors LLP in Birmingham and Swansea.

They all look after us even though we are not that old yet!

I can rightly say in my own language *"Blessed are those children who look after their parents with heart felt love, sympathy and care in whatever condition they are"*.

I am also blessed to have loving brothers and sisters and extended family who have always been close and supported me through the good times and bad. A slight pain or distress affects us all, like branches of a tree. We are all connected, standing tall throughout storms and hazards with our strong roots. Like the saying, *"United we stand, divided we fall"*.

BANGLADESH NATIONAL ATHEM

My Bengal of gold, I love you,

Forever your skies, your air sets my heart in tune,

As if it were a flute,

In Spring, Oh mother of mine, the fragrance from

Your mango-groves makes me wild with joy,

Ah what a thrill!

In autumn Oh mother of mine,

In the full blossomed paddy fields,

I have seen spread all over sweet smiles!

Oh what a beauty, what shades, what an affection,

And what a tenderness!

What a quilt have you spread at the feet of banyan trees
and along the banks of the rivers!

Oh mother of mine, words from your lips are like nectar
to my ears

Ah what a thrill!

If sadness, Oh Mother of mine, casts a gloom on your
face

My eyes are filled with tears!

NOSTALGIA

On my 80th birthday, my wife and myself had been on a short holiday to Jersey, a beautiful island close to England.

We were somewhat tired, after visiting some interesting places.

We sat together on some deck chairs by the beach. I was telling my wife about the days of the past and some of my stories.

Listening to this, my wife started saying,

"O the lone of rambler of the past,

Part of my soul, rhythm of my heart,

People hated you most,

Undermined you a lot,

But you did not surrender

To the trend of the day

Instead you remained still and sturdy

Ahead lied your future in bright

To suit you right"

And my story continues……..

Printed in Poland
by Amazon Fulfillment
Poland Sp. z o.o., Wrocław
13 September 2022

7f2659e1-3065-4566-91aa-10b17e41b71cR01